# THE
# SWIMMING
# POOL

# THE SWIMMING POOL

### STYLISH AND INSPIRATIONAL IDEAS FOR BUILDING AND DECORATING YOUR POOL

## MARTHA BAKER

TEXT WITH ANNE MARIE CLOUTIER

CLARKSON POTTER/PUBLISHERS
NEW YORK

Published by Clarkson Potter/Publishers, New York, New York.
Member of the Crown Publishing Group, a division of Random House, Inc.
www.crownpublishing.com

CLARKSON N. POTTER is a trademark and POTTER and colophon
are registered trademarks of Random House, Inc.

Printed in China

Design by Jennifer K. Beal

Library of Congress Cataloging-in-Publication Data
Baker, Martha
    The swimming pool : stylish and inspirational ideas for building and decorating
your pool / Martha Baker.
        p.   cm.
1. Swimming pools.   2. Landscape architecture.   I. Title.
TH4763.B34   2005
643'.556—dc22                                            2004008664

ISBN 0-609-61076-7

10  9  8  7  6  5  4  3  2

First Edition

## ACKNOWLEDGMENTS

*The Swimming Pool* is a book packed with enchanting spaces. The offerings are totally unique and the differing styles are endless. The book came to life because so many new and old friends were so generous with their time and their pools. How could I forget Lulu, the bulldog, who insisted on being the focus of a California pool and all the other photographic adventures (I will elaborate later).

Many thanks to Bonnie Levison, who introduced me to Round Hill in Jamaica; to Georgia Welles for offering her wonderful world at Windsor; to Jenny Garragues for sharing the Raynors' Moroccan fantasy; to Bunny Williams for her Greek primitive; and to Debby, Bjorn, Kevin, and Jim for allowing me to design their fabulous pools and outdoor living areas.

I want to thank Andy Karsch and Charlotte Barnes for their constant support and Michelle Smith and Jim Bastardo for their magical images.

Finally, I want to thank my amazing children, Emily, Charlie, Hannah, Jesse, and his wife, Sudie. Their support helped to push me through every stage of this book.

# CONTENTS

# INTRODUCTION

SWIMMING POOLS AREN'T A MODERN INNOVATION BY ANY MEANS. On the contrary, man-made water enclosures, once known as baths, have existed in many parts of the world since ancient times. Romans were luxuriating in them in the second century BC, for example, and in India, the Middle East, and elsewhere, archaeologists have unearthed pool structures more than a thousand years older than that. The word *bath* is a reference to the pool's original purpose of communal cleansing (in Britain, home of the historic spa city of Bath, you will still sometimes hear backyard pools referred to as swimming baths).

After a period of time, however, these often-elaborate "watering holes" had come to be regarded as popular venues for relaxation, recreation, and exercise, as well as important focal points for social and family life—in much the same way as private pools are today.

How do we explain this irresistible urge to capture and confine water for our own personal enjoyment? Whatever their setting, pools seem to fill the space with an energy force that immediately draws our attention, making us intimately aware of what Alexander Pope described as "the genius of the place." But perhaps the most obvious attraction to pools lies in the fact that, of all the elements within a landscape or a garden, water has an aesthetic appeal that connects almost immediately with the emotions. Natural beauty reflected in still water evokes a sense of

OPPOSITE: In the idiom of modern classic, the "swimming bath" becomes a personal statement of luxury and grandeur.

mystery and calm. The sparkle of light on its surface and in its depths rejuvenates the spirit. Whether it's splashing from a fountain, flowing over a shoreline, or, for that matter, lapping against the sides of a swimming pool, who can deny the soothing effects of water's music?

Not so long ago, the pleasure of that particular sound was pretty much reserved for the wealthy. These days, however, the combination of improved materials and streamlined building techniques has resulted in a boom in private outdoor swimming pools. Now what was once regarded as a symbol of great wealth has become almost commonplace. Also, since a well-designed backyard pool significantly increases the value of a home, many homeowners are pushed to build a pool by the incentive of an increased property value.

As a professional landscape designer, I've enjoyed both the pleasure and the challenge of creating a variety of pools and pool areas in many different kinds of settings. But in almost every case, when my clients and I begin the planning stage, they are surprised (not to say overwhelmed) by the sheer amount of detail that has to be considered long before the construction begins.

What function is the pool going to serve? Where should it be sited? How big should it be? What shape? These are only a few of the many questions prospective pool owners have to answer early on if they want to be happy with the final result. Given the sizable investment of a pool, you'll want to get everything right the first time because correcting mistakes may end up costing as much as the estimates for the original construction plans.

With all these thoughts in mind, I offer this book as both a guide and an inspiration to anyone who is planning to build a new pool or to renovate and update an existing one. Because success is so often a matter of attention to detail, I'll begin with a rundown of all the major factors to think about before you start.

ABOVE: Sometimes—as with this hillside pool in St. Barts—the question of placement is self evident.

# FACTORS TO CONSIDER WHEN BUILDING A POOL

## CODES

Rule number one: Plan before you build, and check the local code before you plan. Forty or fifty years ago, people built backyard pools pretty much as they pleased. But after a series of tragic drownings that resulted when young children wandered into unfenced pool areas, precautionary measures were enacted to keep such accidents from happening again. Now every town has pool codes that you'll have to meet before being issued a Certificate of Occupancy. And while most codes are fairly standard, always check with your town's building department to familiarize yourself with its particular requirements. You should also be aware that even if you're renovating an older pool built before codes were in place, you'll have to bring it up to code retroactively.

In addition to standard pool codes, your town may also have an environmental ordinance that prohibits you from draining your pool of water or from using the town's water supply to fill it. In the former case, protectors (like a pool cover) are essential for keeping the water as clean as possible; in the latter, you'll have to buy water from another source and truck it in. Be sure to factor in these additional costs.

## FUNCTION

The first aspect of the planning stages is determining how you're going to use the pool. For example, if you've envisioned your pool as a quiet retreat from faxes, phones, and the daily demands of family life, then you may want to site it as far from the house as your land allows. Conversely, if it's going to function as a recre-

ation center for kids, and a safe place where they can learn to swim, you'll want it close to the house, where you can keep an eye on them. Siting the pool this way might also be the most convenient option if the pool is to be used as an entertaining and dining center for adults, for kids' parties, or as a warm-weather eating area, where you can enjoy an outdoor breakfast or lunch. Or if exercise and swimming laps are high priorities for you, then you'll want a pool that's designed to accommodate that purpose. Whatever function your pool is meant to serve—be it any or all of the above—you'll want to keep it in mind at every step in the planning process.

## SITE

The next decision you'll need to make is where to put the pool. If your space is limited, then the pool will probably be immediately adjacent to the house. But there are good reasons for choosing this option even if your grounds are more spacious. Some people like the idea of the pool area as an extension of the house so that it becomes an additional "room." If the pool is placed next to the house, all of the windows overlooking that space will have a view of the pool. And if it is made an extension of one particular room, like the kitchen, say, activity that goes on there will spill out into the pool area (in warm-weather months, at least). This is something to keep in mind if you expect to use the pool as an entertainment/dining center. Or your pool might serve as the outdoor extension of a living room, master suite, guest suite, or home gym.

For owners of a large property, another option is to put more distance between the house and the pool so that it becomes a "destination point," suggesting a retreat from everyday home activities. This placement is also a good aesthetic ploy for psychologically moving you from one space to a distinctly new area of the property. This could even be a way to put an otherwise idle area to practical use.

OPPOSITE: The close proximity of this pool and hot tub to the house couldn't be more convenient.

Or the pool might serve as a transition space between the house and your property line. Neither cramping the house nor too far away from it, the pool then serves as a focal point that creates a visual punch on the landscape. For some people, hiding the pool or distancing it from the house is also a way to avoid having to look at a covered pool (which may strike them as unattractive) during the colder months.

Some owners prefer to have pools fully exposed to sunlight all through the day or at least during their customary swimming hours. If you're one of them, then you'll want to check for pool-covering shadows from trees, outbuildings, and so on during various times of the day before deciding where to site the pool as well as the surrounding pool area (where chaises, tables, and such might be placed). On the other hand, whether for health reasons or just personal preference, you might like the idea of swimming in a shaded pool with sunlight filtering through the leaves of a tree and dappling the water. If so, then place or landscape the pool with that in mind.

BELOW: Though this pool area is surrounded by trees, the pool itself is fully exposed to sunlight.

Another choice addresses the matter of gradients. Do you want the level of the pool to be higher than that of the house so that you take a few steps up to get to it, or would you prefer it to be lower so that you step down to reach it? If your land has a natural slope, you may just want to go with the flow of the natural contours so that the pool either sits on a perch overlooking the house and grounds or is sited down below the house so that it serves as a focal point.

There's one final option you might want to consider: If your property overlooks a body of water, whether it's the ocean, a lake, a river, or a bay, you could choose a design that's called an infinity or disappearing edge pool. When this type of pool is situated near a natural body of water, anyone in the pool can look to the natural water and, from the right vantage point, enjoy the illusion of swimming in it, as if the man-made pool and the natural body of water were one and the same. If you do choose an infinity pool sited in this way, you'll want to enhance the illusion by choosing the color of pool-lining material that most closely matches the natural water.

## SIZE AND SHAPE

From the most ancient pools to the latest in modern pool design, the hands-down winner in the shape category has always been the rectangle. Which isn't to say that other options didn't always exist. They did centuries ago, and they are still popular today. A pool can be round, oval, or octagonal. It can be L-shaped, T-shaped, or cross-shaped (all variations of the basic rectangle, as is the curve-ended rectangle that suggests an oval shape). Or it can be free-form, kidney-shaped, or even heart-shaped.

Before letting your imagination run wild, a bit of advice: There's good reason why some of the more unusual shapes are so rarely, if ever, seen. Some of them are impractical for swimming (lap swimming in particular). Some are now considered

ABOVE: The long sides of this oversized, oval-shaped pool are broken up by boxed-out areas that provide built-in niches for square containers.

ABOVE: A rectangular pool might be notched at the corners and curved at one (or both) ends.

ABOVE: Three rectangular pools break up the vast lawn and provide a sleek symmetry to the space, creating a geometric sculpture.

old-fashioned (like the kidney shape so reminiscent of the 1950s and '60s), kitschy (like heart-shaped pools associated with honeymoon resorts), or simply unappealing (like the rounds and octagonals, which remind people of prefab aboveground pools). These popular modern sensibilities are worth keeping in mind because the shape and general appeal of your pool could have a direct bearing on your property's resale value.

The rectangle, the most practical and traditional pool shape, is the most popular. As the nation has become more health- and exercise-conscious, a phenomenon that swelled following World War II, people began to appreciate swimming as a particularly beneficial form of exercise, which led to the building of more and more rectangular pools.

In the 1950s, when land, water, and just about everything cost a lot less than they do now, the average pool was 25 by 50 feet. Then as prices rose and the typical acreage of properties shrunk, the standard was reduced to 20 by 40 feet (which still holds today). With the resurgence of health-consciousness in the 1980s and '90s, lap swimmers began to realize that length, not width, was the most important consideration, and soon lap pools were the rage. While these elongated rectangles might be even less than 40 feet long (or short-lap measure), their narrow width (usually 8 to 10 feet) makes them look longer.

Also worth mentioning in this regard is the fact that pool manufacturers figure cost by a pool's square footage. So even if you reduce the width and extend the length of the standard 20-by-40-foot pool, the price will generally remain the same.

The lap pool's elongated shape is reminiscent of traditional pools found in Moorish water gardens, where a long trough of water continuously spills out into a wider pool. Today some pool designers are doing modern takeoffs on that basic idea.

If you want to swim laps for exercise but your space is very limited, you may want to consider a motorized pool where, in a space as small as 8 by 15 feet, you can swim in place against a speed-adjustable current and get a terrific workout. Though such a pool is primarily designed for indoor use, your builder may be able to suggest ways of adapting it for the outdoors.

Another version of the rectangle, and to me the most elegant, is the oval-shaped pool like one I once saw in northern Michigan. Long and straight-sided, it still served the same function as a rectangle, but because the short ends were curved, it looked softer, more natural, and much less sharp-edged.

If you want your pool to look as natural as possible, there's the free-form pool, which, when properly landscaped, can make you think you're swimming in a natural lagoon. If judiciously planned by a pro so that the water is surrounded by plantings of trees and shrubs that hide the property's boundaries from view, this kind of pool can create the illusion of making even a small piece of land look as if it goes on forever (as you'll see for yourself in "The Rustic Pool").

## SPAS

The hot tub—or spa, as it's now more commonly called—is becoming increasingly popular for a number of reasons. These small enclosures of heated water and muscle-soothing, pulsating jets were originally prized solely for their therapeutic value. However, they have gradually become focal points for socializing, and they're being used more and more for heating up after a brisk dip in an unheated pool. The shallow water level and confined space of a spa also make it the perfect vehicle for introducing toddlers to water or just for relaxing while holding a little one in your lap.

The newest spas are usually square or rectangular. They can be found near the pool, attached to it, or within it. They might also have a fountainlike feature that spurts water into the pool, thereby adding the sound and sight of falling water to the pleasure of a pool.

## POOL ACCESS

Way back when, getting in and out of the pool involved negotiating a ladder attached to the side. Today, however, the more common means of access involves a series of steps, which, in practical and visual terms, is a great improvement. Some placement options to consider: A rectangle might have steps running across one short side at the shallow end of the pool. For an oval-shaped pool, steps could be placed at the corners where the ends of the long sides meet the ends of the shorter sides. I once designed a linear pool with steps all along one side like stadium seating, enabling people to sit and talk while enjoying the cool of the water. This is a particularly good way to handle step placement for a lap pool, where swimmers need straight end-walls for the flip-turn/push-off maneuver (which they couldn't do if steps were there). If your pool is adjacent to a terrace, you might want the pool steps to lead directly down from the terrace and into the water. The options are almost endless, but most often your choice for pool access will be dictated by the shape of your pool, its function, and the design of the adjoining patio and pool area.

## FENCES AND GATES

Fences and gates are probably the most important requirements covered by your town's pool code. Generally, your pool or pool area must be enclosed with a fence that's at least 4 feet high, and its gates must have a particular kind of childproof latch that only an adult can open (by reaching over the top of the fence and unlatching it from the inside).

ABOVE: A protective gate might top a set of steps leading to the pool area.

ABOVE: The semicircular steps and angular railing introduce a lovely aesthetic dimension to a functional purpose.

But if for aesthetic reasons you're not particularly happy with the idea of a fenced-in pool, there are ways of meeting fencing requirements that are still aesthetically viable. For example, you might have an infinity pool where a fence would obstruct the view between the pool and the natural body of water it overlooks. In that case, you could elevate the pool so it's 4 feet above the ground and fence off the access steps leading up to it. Still another option for avoiding that fenced-in feeling: You could fence the perimeter of your entire property, which will satisfy code requirements as long as there are gates at each entryway. A less expensive solution in this case would be to enclose a larger area surrounding the pool. Or if you want to create the cozy sense of an outdoor "room," then site the fence fairly close to the pool paving. If privacy is an issue, the fence might be as high as 8 feet so that the pool area becomes a personal space, like a secret garden. But do remember this rule of thumb: The more solid the fence ("solid" includes densely growing plant materials as well as wooden fences with narrow spaces or no spacing between the uprights), the farther it should be from the pool area. Otherwise, it won't allow for the free flow of air to the enclosed area, which is key to avoiding the heat that could make swimmers and loungers uncomfortable.

From a purely aesthetic point of view, the type of fence you choose should be in keeping with the style of your house and property or with the style of the pool. For a modern pool, you'd want sleek and minimalistic fencing, like Plexiglas panels set into metal posts or a guy-wire type of arrangement with steel posts. For a classic

ABOVE: A good choice for a classical fence is a stone balustrade softened by jasmine vine.

OPPOSITE: Within one growth season, this hornbeam hedge will grow straight through the fence, hiding its cyclone wiring.

pool, you might choose brick, stone, stuccoed walls, or a trellised fence (which, like the picket fence, would also work well with a pool of the romantic style).

People who don't like the look of a fence or wall around the pool often use a simple chain-link or deer-wire fence and then sandwich it between two rows of hedges made of privet or evergreens or similar types of plants. (Hedges alone won't satisfy pool codes.) Another option is to cover a wire fence with vines, climbing hydrangeas, or climbing roses, which will soften the look of the fence and eventually hide it from view completely. This is also a good way to hide an unattractive metal fence. Lastly, if the pool is adjacent to the house, the house itself might be considered a "fence" for one side of the pool.

Given all of the above options, the type of fencing you choose doesn't have to be an either/or situation. Quite often a combination of different types can be used very successfully to satisfy code requirements and your personal design sense.

When the pool area is created as an outdoor room with fencing around its immediate perimeter, the gate becomes the door leading into it and, as such, you'll want it to have as much visual impact as the door to your house. The gate could be taller or more elaborate than the fence. It might be topped by a pergola or an arched arbor to give the sense of a ceiling as you pass through the gate. Just as a front door might be flanked by a pair of urns filled with plant arrangements, so could a pool gate. The same effect can be created with a pair of statues, sculptures, or other decorative features to welcome visitors entering the pool area.

ABOVE: This custom lattice fence with unusual curve details is made more solid with two layers of offset lattice. The curved top of the fence prevents it from becoming too imposing a barrier.

## POOL MATERIAL

Pool material is the visible facing of a pool that covers its floor and walls. Nowadays the pool material of choice is Gunite, a concoction of marble dust and other ingredients that's power-sprayed onto a wooden pool frame. Though expensive, it's very durable and comes in a wide range of color (which makes it especially suitable for, say, an infinity pool, where you want the shade closest to the color of the natural water just beyond the pool).

Another pool material option is poured concrete, though it isn't commonly used anymore, particularly in northern areas, because it tends to crack from the freezing and thawing conditions that characterize cold-weather climates. It's also slippery when wet. In the 1980s and '90s, some pools were faced with a molded plastic liner that felt and looked artificial. One point in favor of plastic liners is that they are fairly inexpensive compared with Gunite and concrete. On the other hand, if expense is not a concern, you might want to face your pool with beautiful tiles, which was done in the Moroccan-style pool shown in "The Romantic Pool."

ABOVE: A lovely rock garden climbing up toward a crest of trees also serves as a safety fence.

## COPING

Coping is the area (usually 1 to 2 feet wide) immediately surrounding the pool, typically on all sides. It is commonly thought of as the frame of a pool. Some people prefer coping that's made of the same material as the patio but perhaps set in a different pattern so that the contrast between the two is minimal. Others may even do without coping altogether so that the patio itself wraps around the pool's perimeter. But to really define the pool shape and visually make it "pop," the coping should be either a different color than the patio or a different material entirely. Some good choices for coping include bluestone, slate, granite, limestone, brick—even grass. You might also consider elevating the coping to create a low wall that really makes

the pool stand out from the surrounding lawn or patio and also provides seating around the pool.

## PAVING AND PATIOS

Paving is used to define the patio area, whether it completely surrounds the pool or is confined to a smaller area adjoining only one side of it. Instead of paving, grass can be used, which eliminates the hot-foot syndrome caused by most types of paving and allows for a simplified progression of lawn/coping/pool. Perhaps you consider paving essential for defining the area where chaises, tables, and other pool accessories reside. If you do decide to go that route, you have the option of elevating the patio to add another level—and an additional element of visual interest—to a rectangular pool, while giving chaise loungers a better view of the pool area.

Other commonly used patio materials include brick (a true magnet for heat) and wooden decking (which is cooler but requires maintenance to keep it from splintering). Bluestone is a better-looking alternative, but its drawback is that it's particularly hot under bare feet. After doing some research for a pool I was working on in Long Island, New York, I discovered a shop called South-ampton Brick & Tile that has a paler-hued type of bluestone from India called Blue Ice, which isn't nearly as hot on the feet as the common variety.

One of my favorite paving materials is limestone, which, because of its pale color, never seems to overheat. Though it is very expensive, I think it's the most beautiful choice. If you live in the North, here's something to remember if you choose a limestone patio: Be sure to buy Canadian limestone, which is fit to withstand freezing temperatures, as opposed to Arizona limestone, which doesn't have that capability.

When designing a patio area, be sure to provide a generous amount of space for chaises (which can measure more than 6 feet long when in full reclining position), as well as additional space for comfortably walking around them.

If entertaining will be an integral part of your poolside life, you'll also need a designated space for a dining table and chairs, a serving table, and whatever else you think it necessary.

## SUN SHELTERS

With people spending so much more of their time around the pool, they want more sun protection than what is offered by the typical umbrella (which barely shades more than the chaise beneath it). One good sun-shelter idea is an arbor or a pergola covered with plants such as wisteria, climbing hydrangeas, deciduous vines, evergreens, and so on. Solid roof structures with open sides are also popular, as are open-sided tents (some of which are elaborate enough to double as outdoor living and dining rooms).

If the pool is next to the house, you could have a mechanized retractable canvas awning attached to it so that by pressing a button the awning opens over the patio area to produce complete shade or closes when you want full sun.

## POOL HOUSES

The basic cabana has not simply grown over the years, but it has truly come into its own. These days, a pool house might be anything from an open-sided hut to a miniature replica of the family home. Aside from functioning as the ultimate sun shelter, a pool house can be used as a changing room, a meditation room, a living room, a dining room, a kitchen, a bathroom—even a guest room.

Most often, pool houses are used for entertaining, including dining. To cater to that need, you might have a minikitchen outfitted with a stove, a convection oven, a rotisserie, a grill, a fridge and an ice-maker, and a sink and storage cabinets—all made of rustproof

stainless steel. As you explore all of the possibilities for a fully equipped kitchen, you'll find that several top-name manufacturers of stoves and other appliances are now making models especially designed for pool house and outdoor use.

Some pool houses have washers and dryers to manage the seemingly constant pileup of wet towels and swimsuits. Some have the convenience of powder rooms and showers (indoor or out). Nowadays quite a few of them also have fireplaces, which not only reinforce the feel of a living room but also make them cozy settings for lounging or entertaining on cool summer nights. (This holds true even when the fireplace is outdoors, under the stars.)

If you find yourself planning the ultimate pool house, remember to factor in the installation of whatever utility lines may be needed to service the amenities you choose for it. Also, the more elaborate you want the pool house to be, the more you'll need a design that can be effectively closed up and locked during the off-season.

## POOL EQUIPMENT

One last convenience afforded by a pool house: All of the necessary (yet noisy and unattractive) pool equipment, like generators and filters, can be hidden behind it. If that isn't enough, you can camouflage the workings completely by surrounding them with a trellis or enclosing them inside their own little pool-equipment house. A final idea for hiding the equipment is to elevate the pool and install the equipment beneath it within a surrounding wall with access doors.

## FURNITURE

Furniture may include several chaises as well as tables and chairs. If you entertain often, you might also want a buffet or serving table. For those who like the idea of creating a real outdoor living room (particularly in a pool house), the list could also include big, cushy club chairs and sofas positioned around a coffee table. Whatever furniture pieces you choose, they should be in keeping with the style of the pool area, whether it's romantic, modern, classic, or rustic.

Teak furniture, which is solid and durable, is very popular now. Some people like to let it naturally age to a soft, weathered-gray color. To prevent teak from getting splintery, I stain it with something called Chemcoat, which acts as a sealer and gives it a nice smooth mahogany-toned finish. (The only drawback is that to maintain the finish you'll have to sand it and recoat it every year or so.) Another good choice for pool furniture is cast aluminum, which is lightweight and, unlike standard aluminum, rustproof. Wrought iron and steel are two more rustproof options to consider. Or how about stone? I've designed a limestone table for a number of clients using a slab of limestone cut to size and finished with a smooth or a rough edge. It then becomes a tabletop for a decorative stone base. As it ages, the weatherproof limestone gets a wonderful patina, and the table adds a nice sculptural element to the pool area.

ABOVE: Pool equipment is often hidden behind shrubs. This clever alternative has slatted doors for ventilation and a roof that echoes that of the house.

ABOVE: A very simple solution for poolside relaxation is a pair of Adirondack chairs.

OPPOSITE: Not only does this pool house provide shade, its arched openings on three sides create great ventilation and provide wonderful views of the nearby harbor.

Most of the chairs you buy will come with cushions made with a Sunbrella fabric that dries quickly, resists stains, and withstands heavy use. When I choose furniture for clients, I always recommend that they also buy heavy vinyl covers that can be ordered from a catalog. They come in a nice shade of gray-green, and the beauty is that you can toss them over cushioned chairs (and other furniture pieces) instead of putting them in storage if you're going to be away for a few weeks. Even though Sunbrella fabric is weatherproof, it will still last longer and look better if you protect it from the elements when the pool area isn't in use.

## STORAGE CONTAINERS

While you're leafing through pool furniture catalogs, don't forget about storage containers to hold such pool paraphernalia as sun umbrellas, floating devices, and furniture cushions during the winter months or vinyl furniture covers during the swimming season. For pool parties, a galvanized wooden container would be a handy holder for cold drinks and free up the fridge for comestibles. Whether fashioned from teak, marine plywood, or other waterproof material, storage containers should be weather-tight to avoid mildew and keep the contents dry. When attractively designed, these poolside boxes do double duty as serving tables, while also providing extra seating.

## LANDSCAPING

Plants add color, sculptural interest, and a much-needed vertical element to a horizontal pool area, while introducing a natural softness to counter the hard-edged outlines of furniture, fences, and other man-made features. By planting trees a short distance from the pool area, you can create an oasislike shelter from the sun. Or you might want to plant trees close to the pool in order to shade it (but if you do, be prepared to deal with fallen leaves and other natural debris).

For many people, the pool area is an ideal place for a garden, not only because of its natural color and beauty but also because it enables people to do garden work and still be a part of any poolside activity that's going on. You might plant rose beds there, create a sculptural parterre with annuals mixed in among geometric shapes of boxwood, or grow a classic perennial garden or *potager* (kitchen garden).

Another landscaping choice is the low-maintenance potted garden, where manicured shrubs and colorful annuals are planted in large wooden containers or graceful urns strategically placed to enhance the look of the pool area. When you select plants and containers that reflect the style of the pool, they'll complement that style. For example, beautiful old urns would be perfect for a romantic setting. For a classic pool, you might use slatted wood containers (often called Versailles boxes) with hinged sides and wheels of industrial-strength construction designed to hold small trees. One advantage to this container type is that in cooler climates you can display tropical plants such as palms in summer, then wheel them into a temperature-controlled storage space during the off-season. For a more rustic feel, plant containers might be made out of twigs or even a retro material like *faux bois* (cement that is made to look like wood). If your pool style is modern, you could have custom-made mahogany planters or sleek steel containers holding seemingly geometric, angular plants.

## LIGHTING

On warm summer nights, the pool area is an ideal place to be, and whether you're swimming, lounging, or entertaining, you'll need proper lighting. Lights inside the pool create a subterranean fantasy that delights the eye and stirs the imagination. When there's a party going on, you'll want to illuminate the patio to avoid mishaps (like a pair of dancers accidentally falling into the pool). In addition, you may want to uplight a nearby tree, or plant several spotlights to showcase the garden. For a dining area, you could hang lanterns from a pergola or the roof of the pool house. Or you could staple a string of old-fashioned miniglobe lights to the beams of a pergola for festive and soft lighting. Another way to go is to burn big canister-shaped candles inside large glass hurricane lamps that will protect them from passing breezes. Many people like the effect of tall Polynesian torches planted in various locations surrounding the patio. My own personal favorites are ball-shaped torches of stainless steel or cast iron.

## HEATING AND COVERING THE POOL

Cost may dictate your decision to heat your pool. Although many people have stopped heating their pool because of the increasing cost, I'm seeing more and more people start to turn on the heat simply because they don't like swimming in the pool unless it's warm. And, of course, having a heated pool also means that you can use the pool when the weather is cool.

One way to harness the heat that pool water naturally stores from sunlight is to cover the pool at night. A popular cover used for storing heat is the automatic device that uses an insulated material called Thinsulate. With the press of a button, the Thinsulate cover unwinds from its container and runs along tracks installed on each long side of the pool to cover it. This is a good safety device to prevent small children from falling into the pool when the area is not in use. If you happen to live in an area where you're not permitted to drain a pool, covering it at night is one way of keeping the pool water cleaner for a longer period of time.

## A FINAL WORD

My last bit of advice is to go through every heading you've just read and make a list of your nonnegotiables—the elements that are top priority for you—then work with your pool designer to come up with the most satisfactory ways of making adjustments to accommodate that must-have list. And if you're looking for examples to inspire those ideas, just feast your eyes on the wonderful pools featured on the upcoming pages.

# R

ROMANTIC

# THE ROMANTIC POOL

If evening entertaining figures high on your priorities list, the romantic pool can set a mood for festivity and fantasy that will

beguile your guests even before the first cork is popped. Creating that effect is a lot like designing a stage set, where the desired atmosphere or sense of place is first established by the structural elements of the pool area itself, then reinforced with color, lighting, furnishings, and botanicals.

When planning a patio, for example, think in terms of space for an exotic serving tent or a cozy outdoor living room with a fireplace, sofas, and low tables, where guests can gather for drinks and conversation. Or imagine your candlelit dinner table in a filmy-curtained gazebo or under a vine-covered pergola festooned with strings of little sparkling lights.

The theater set you fashion might be vividly stimulating or seductively elegant. It may conjure anything from an English garden to a Spanish courtyard. In short, the romantic pool is the stage for fantasy— whatever yours may be.

**ABOVE:** The softness and colors of flowers, like these canna lilies, accentuate the mood of romantic style.

**OPPOSITE:** In tropical climates like St. Barts, top-hinged shutters on poolside houses admit cooling breezes and filter sunlight.

# A TROPICAL EDEN

When people speak of "an island paradise" they could well be describing the French West Indian isle of Saint Barthélemy (or as it's more commonly known, St. Barts), the location of the property-cum-infinity pool that you see here. Owned by Parisian photographer Patrick Demarchelier, it's situated high on a hillside overlooking the shops and sailboats of Gustavia Harbour, which some assert is one of the best views on the island.

In this setting, the living quarters are made up of a series of interconnected structures—each serving a specific function. One is used for cooking and dining. One serves as a living room. Several provide sleeping quarters for the owner and his guests.

The overall design takes its cue from island tradition. Roof-lines are pyramidal in shape. Colors borrow from a bright Caribbean palette of sea greens and sunshine yellows. Windows are shutters that swing outward to take advantage of every cooling breeze.

Here furniture tends to be casual, minimal, and varied. On a walkway outside of one room, for example, you might come across a little bistro arrangement of a table and two weathered chairs; on the patio you'll find a few white-cushioned chaises and a collection of exercise mats all grouped together like unusually soft flooring.

For garden interest, the hillside provides palm trees and a hundred species of flowers and plants that make the word *lush* seem woefully inadequate. Add spectacular sunsets viewed from a poolside chaise, and what you have is a pretty accurate description of, well, an island paradise.

OPPOSITE: Cushioned wooden chaises are perfectly positioned for loungers to enjoy the idyllic view.

ABOVE: The infinity pool seems to float above the vivid expanse of Gustavia Harbour.

**LEFT:** Palm trees and pyramid rooftop make striking silhouettes against an early-evening sky.

**RIGHT:** A bevy of boats and a yacht two are familiar sights in the waters of Gustavia Harbour.

ABOVE: A roofed shelter near the pool is equipped with a table and benches for casual dining.

LEFT: When needed, a series of adjustable shutters can provide sun protection for a raised-platform terrace.

BELOW: As the day progresses, wheeled chaises allow poolside loungers to follow the sunny (or shady) patches with ease.

# TUDOR-STYLE TRANQUILLITY

The Tudor cottage–style house in this romantic Hamptons, New York, setting inspires the mood for everything in the pool area adjacent to it—starting with the pool itself. The shape is essentially oval, but on both sides of the shorter end-curves, the oval is notched to accommodate little sets of access steps, an arrangement that adds an almost Elizabethan sense of refinement and elegance.

In the Tudor household, individual furniture pieces were often designed to serve several functions, and the pool area's surrounding wall recalls that same tradition. In terms of necessity, it's a security fence. But because the property is next to the ocean, it also serves as a protective break from offshore winds. In addition, this lovely brick wall with its wood-shingled coping creates a vertical element that's an ideal support for the climbing roses and other old-fashioned plant materials growing in the garden.

When the pool is empty of swimmers, the owners simply enjoy watching how the still water reflects the light and landscape. In part for that purpose, the pool was ornamented with an exquisite sculptural nymph encircled by two spouting dolphins and with coping-supported pots overflowing with flowers and vines that create the illusion of repeating themselves in the water's reflection as they arch over the edge of the pool.

As a whole, each element helps to create a lush, intimate space that defines romantic style at its most elegant.

OPPOSITE: The statue of a water maid presides over the pool's reflection of the Tudor-style cottage.

ABOVE: From the house steps, viewers can take in the entire pool area and its surrounding garden wall.

**ABOVE:** Poolside vignettes like this one beautifully demonstrate the appeal of romantic style.

**BELOW:** Clean lined and ruggedly graceful, the Japanese-style lantern perfectly suits its setting.

**RIGHT:** The neat angle of the notched oval pool shape offers an ideal place for access steps.

**LEFT:** When lit, candles embedded in a pot of ivy will add flickering light to evening swims.

**RIGHT:** An open door in the enclosure wall gives a tantalizing glimpse of pool and garden.

**ABOVE:** The shingle-coped brick wall fends off ocean winds and supplies a picturesque vertical for climbing roses.

**LEFT:** Burgeoning from a ceramic container, verbena and sweet potato vines spill their images into the pool.

# MOROCCAN GRANDEUR

The dreamy theme of this exquisite pool in southeastern Florida was inspired by a passion for Morocco, a place the owners know quite well. Upon entering the property through a brightly painted door from the street, visitors are instantly charmed by the Aladdin's cave of architectural nuances they find along the walkway to the pool. Beyond the door, they pass through a little wrought-iron gate, while looking underfoot at the squares of coral stone etched with a kaleidoscope of color-patterned pebbles and tiles.

The pool area is found just outside the house, where blue-framed doors leading from the master suite open onto it. In place of a pool house, there's a spacious Moroccan tent partially enclosing a large round table and a curved banquette used for dining. Even the tent's intricately designed furnishings, such as lamps, side tables, and other accent pieces, all reflect the same North African influence.

Part of the setting's dreamlike quality comes from the lavish use of tropical poolside plantings, including some palm trees (hand-selected by the pool's architect, Dennis la Marche), which swoop out over the water and transform the strong Florida sun into soft dappling shadows.

Set against this lush background are lanterns, fringed white umbrellas, and, flanking the access steps in a little square offshoot of the linear pool, a pair of reclining stone elephants. Everything you see sparks the interest, pleases the eye, and conjures all the mystery and delight of a Middle Eastern souk.

LEFT: The designs on a large earthenware jug replicate those used in Moroccan carpets.

RIGHT: Ceramic tile laid in a herringbone pattern lines the floor of the pool.

OPPOSITE: The lushness of curving palms and spurting water arcs turn a Florida pool into a private oasis.

LEFT: At the pool's street-side entrance, yellow shutters and a distinctive gate create a bright welcome.

BELOW LEFT: On the tent wall, a Moroccan mirror hangs between two serving-table lamps.

BELOW: Umbrella poles set into stone elephants instead of typical umbrella bases add an exotic touch to the pool area.

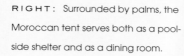

RIGHT: Surrounded by palms, the Moroccan tent serves both as a pool-side shelter and as a dining room.

BELOW: An appropriately Moorish-style door is framed by tiled columns and flanked by large ceramic jars.

/E: Just beyond the dining tent, water steps descend into the pool.

DW: Glass lanterns with inverted-tops sprout from plantings alongside thway.

**ABOVE:** An alligator adds whimsy and creates an unusual focal point at one end of the pool.

**LEFT:** The juxtaposition of herringbone tile patterns, coral stone coping, and Moroccan tiles forms a striking combination.

**RIGHT:** Moroccan lanterns lining the pool make for a romantic nighttime setting.

**BELOW:** The guest quarters alongside the pool are set off by an inviting furniture arrangement and a fabulous mosaic.

## PAVING

In the 1950s, most pool patios were made of poured concrete or, for the stylishly ambitious, variegated flagstones. Over the years, as pools became more popular, designers (as well as pool owners) were inspired to create a stunning array of flooring effects, often by using familiar materials in unexpected ways. Today there's an extraordinary number of style choices, ranging in cost from inexpensive (such as pavers of poured cement or composite) to through-the-roof (an entire patio floor design made of hand-set mosaic tiles).

My best advice: Opt for materials that will not become slippery when wet and will stay comparatively cool underfoot, even in direct sun. Choose what will best fit in with or help establish your overall style vision. Keep a sense of balance. For example, if you've fallen in love with a paving design that's very colorful and busy, then make it the major design feature and keep all other elements (furniture, fencing, and so on) subdued and simple. Conversely, if other patio features are on the ornate side, you'll want to go with a

paving color and layout scheme that provide a nice backdrop without competing for attention.

I strongly suggest that before making a final decision, you take the time to look around and consider as many options as you can find—starting with the examples shown here.

Let's take a look at a few of those options. Concrete used as paving material for pool areas has had some bad press over the years. This is chiefly because it's often laid

extensively but unimaginatively so that the result is just a solid expanse of dull gray. But when it's framed with some contrasting material (such as grass, bricks, tiles, shells, stones, or railway ties), concrete can be very attractive. When it's smooth, concrete can also be slippery—a problem that's easily solved by adding some textured material when the concrete's being mixed or by creating a pattern with a trowel to add texture to the surface. As for color, "gray" can mean any one of a range of more than forty pig-

ment variations. Bluestone is a popular choice for pool paving because of its neutral color and availability.

Brick is both great-looking and nonslip, and because of its shape, it can be set flat or on edge and laid out in herringbones, basket-weaves, stack bonds, or running bonds. Old brick has a wonderfully mellow quality, but unfortunately it doesn't hold up well over time. Your best bet would be to buy long-lasting new bricks that have been tumbled to look old.

Timber decking constructed of woods like

Western red cedar or American pitch pine, though totally slip-proof when wet, is on the pricey side. An alternative might be cheaper-grade wood that you can stain or paint.

Paving slabs are often flame-textured, which means that a torch has been fired over them to make the surface slightly uneven, thus improving their grip underfoot. Tip: Paver slabs of French limestone, which are nonporous, are less likely to encourage the growth of slippery algae.

# SPANISH-STYLE MAKEOVER

This is the story of a pool in transition, and it begins in 1920s California. At that time, Spanish colonial–style houses were sprouting up all over the state, and this Hillsborough hacienda was one of them. Then, sometime in the 1960s, thinking (quite rightly) that this was the perfect setting for a pool, someone (quite wrongly) installed an incongruous free-form pool, which was also poorly sited on the property.

When the present owners bought the property, they vowed to eventually renovate the entire pool area. But they preferred to wait before doing the renovation, and they asked me to perform a cosmetic makeover to get them through the interim. When I arrived, most of the old, neglected plants had already been removed, so the "before" picture that remained was simply the barren pool, far too much 1960s-style patio paving, and pathways of unattractive, artificial-looking red tile.

The "after" is what you see here. With half of the paving jackhammered out, the patio is romanticized and partially camouflaged by garden beds filled with a whole range of tropical beauties that thrive in the Golden State. The plants that didn't fit in beds were planted into wonderful Mexican earthenware pots—around the pool, in newly forged sitting areas, and along the walkways of fieldstone that replaced the old red tiles.

The moral of the story: When major renovations have to wait, make-do measures—and especially a generous addition of foliage—can perform wonders to create a pool that you can be happy with in the meantime.

OPPOSITE: A palm tree grows in a large earthenware pot with an elevated metal holder to facilitate drainage.

ABOVE: A trio of soaring palms helps filter sunlight around a California pool.

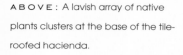

**ABOVE:** A lavish array of native plants clusters at the base of the tile-roofed hacienda.

**RIGHT:** Even Lulu, the family pet, gets a lot of use out of the pool.

**BELOW:** A close-up reveals the dramatic beauty in a single leaf of the Tropicana plant.

**LEFT:** A wall-hung iron plant holder supports a whole colony of thriving succulents.

**RIGHT:** Festively colored canna lilies border the new fieldstone walkway.

**LEFT:** The ghostly image of a leaf-within-a-leaf is characteristic of the Tibouchina heteromalla.

**BELOW:** Potted cypress trees frame the path to a Spanish-style pool house with a dining area, a bar, and a bathroom.

**ABOVE:** This "bud cluster" on a southern magnolia is actually what remains after the tree sheds its flowers.

**ABOVE:** A glazed celadon pot makes an ideal container for palmy leaves and little "hens and chicks."

**BELOW:** Green spears of Maori Queen add another interesting texture and shape to the plant mix.

**ABOVE:** A flowering Tropicana is just one of many plant varieties that thrive in California's subtropical climate.

**LEFT:** Dewdrops glitter on small purple blooms of a 6-foot-high Tibouchina.

**ABOVE LEFT:** Decorative iron benches and a table create an inviting conversation spot near the pool area.

**ABOVE:** Euphorbia is a very popular plant material in England that makes for an unusual choice for a California garden, offering an air of classicism to play against the tropical theme.

**LEFT:** Succulent "hens and chicks" add an unexpected touch to poolside planting.

# IN THE EUROPEAN TRADITION

In the subtropical climate of Florida, a swimming pool is pretty much sine qua non for the average home. So when plans were being drawn up for this luxury resort community on the state's eastern coast, the developers made sure that every house was supplied with a pool.

Like most of the community's homes, the design of this residence was inspired by European examples that surround a central courtyard. Houses like this one enclose a pool on three sides, with the fourth side open to a spectacular view, in

this case, a freshwater pond. With such a prospect practically on his doorstep, the owner's natural choice was an infinity pool, which, at 12 by 45 feet, is tailor-made for swimming laps.

The patio made of French limestone is a classic take on romantic style. Uncluttered and utterly simple, it has little more than a few polished teak chairs and chaises by way of furnishings. To soften that classic simplicity, there are feathery palm trees that seem to turn sunlight into moving shadows sprinkled with gold, and at the far end of the pool is a sculptured metal dragon breathing tongues of fire into the balmy Florida night. All of these elements are very romantic indeed.

ABOVE: Positioned in the courtyard and punctuated with a gorgeous sculptural piece, the pool essentially becomes a part of the house itself.

OPPOSITE: The lit dragon creates a spectacular focal point and sets a truly magical scene.

# LUSH RETREAT

What I especially love about this romantic Hamptons hideaway in New York is the juxtaposition of the T-shaped pool and the shelter. With just the narrowest strip of bluestone patio separating the two, they seem almost like a single entity so that you could conceivably just roll out of bed (the shelter is furnished for sleeping) and, with a few steps, be in the water doing morning laps.

Since the owner wanted the pool shelter to double as a pergola, the pedimented roof is latticed to provide an anchor for a lush blanket of fragrant wisteria. Down

below are additional softening touches, like the ceiling-hung swath of netting that drapes over the bed, some cushy upholstered footstools, and a comfy rattan wing chair. To provide a little extra warmth (and a pleasant gathering spot) for late-night swim parties, there's a wonderful fireplace made of the same bluestone as the shelter's front columns, which plunge right down into the pool.

But perhaps the most romantic aspect of this pool is the setting itself. Surrounded by a meadow-sized carpet of lawn encircled by trees, it has a great sense of privacy, and promotes the feeling of existing within a world complete in itself.

OPPOSITE: Steps lead directly from the pool house into the water, blurring the distinction between the two elements.

ABOVE: A shelter abuts an L-shaped pool with a horizontal length of 35 feet, playing against its 75-foot length.

**ABOVE:** The dramatic reflection of the pool house is heightened by the pool's elongated shape.

**BELOW:** From the shelter's vantage point, there's a clear view of the T-shaped pool surrounded by lawn and trees.

**ABOVE:** The pool house doubles as a guest room. How inviting is it to get out of bed and jump in the pool before you've had your morning coffee?

ABOVE: The round umbrella and curved dining patio create a geometric interplay with the horizontal line of the pool.

LEFT: Within its open, columned walls, the shelter is as graciously furnished as an indoor living room.

# THE ROMANCE OF RED

The moment that decorator Scott Sanders was shown this assignment in Southampton, New York, he saw red—a racy fire-engine red played against splashes of white. The inspiration for his color palette was the pool's redbrick patio, and the occasion was the 2003 showcase presentation sponsored by *House & Garden* at the Hamptons Designer Show House.

With the pool, patio, and tent structure already in place (as is often the case with

a newly bought property), this was purely a makeover job, and Sanders approached it with gusto. His first step was to replace the tent's canvas with broad panels of red and white fabrics to shelter a cozy dining area. Then, to create the sense of a real outdoor room, he established its farthest boundary with white wood lattice walls springing outward from each side of the tent and furnished the aforementioned brick patio with all the comforts of a conventional living room.

As you'd expect, the fabric cushion covers for that furniture reflect the color scheme, but they do it in a lighthearted and unexpected way. The chaise, sofa, and back pillow of one chair are red with white piping, one chair seat cushion is red with red piping, and the other two are white with red piping.

The red-painted box containers for the poolside topiaries are of Sanders's own design (a case of necessity giving birth to invention when he couldn't find any ready-mades he liked). And the pièce de résistance: two giant blow-up lobsters floating in the center of the pool.

ABOVE: Like hearts and roses, red says romance— as does the setting for this delightful pool.

OPPOSITE: The unexpected brilliant red of the peaked roof tent and humorous lobsters create a great vista from the house.

# FURNITURE

Poolside living isn't just about swimming. It also means stretching out to read a good book or take a nap, enjoying drinks and leisurely talks, and gathering together for simple meals and festive parties. In fact, the pool/patio area is an outdoor room that serves many of the same functions as the family rooms inside your house. When choosing furniture for it, the same considerations will always apply.

Take style, for example. Patio furniture is often the most powerful element in establishing the pool style you want to create. Many use its design and color to determine their choices for other elements, such as fencing, awnings, and ornaments.

In addition to good looks, think comfort. Is a dining chair a comfortable height for the table? Is the table big enough to accommodate extra guests? Some peo-

ple prefer the softness of cushioned chairs and chaises. If you're one of them, you'll also have to think about where to store the cushions in the winter months. Or you might opt for styles without cushions, with seats that are woven or made of open-worked construction that allows for the cooling effect of air circulation. Whichever you choose, test for comfort before you buy.

Convenience is another consideration. For example, in addition to a dining table, you'll want tables alongside chaises and chairs for holding drinks and such. A storage container with a minifridge for ice and cold drinks is also a handy patio addition, particularly if you don't have a pool house with kitchen facilities. Some of these outdoor cabinets are made of wood and are actually quite handsome furniture pieces. Also, do think about the multiuse factor. For example, the top of a standing storage container might double as a preparation or serving table. Sturdy, four-legged stools (with or without cushions) could work as ottomans, extra seating, or handy surfaces for setting drink trays upon.

Last, but most certainly not least, is the matter of sheer practicality. Aside from being able to withstand hard wear and weather, patio furniture like chairs and chaises should be light enough to be easily moved but sturdy enough to stay put on gusty days. If your pool is near a natural body of water and open to offshore winds, then sturdy becomes the top priority. In that regard, an open-worked design (sans cushions) is often better because breezes flow through it rather than push against it. Generally, cast aluminum is a good choice because, though lighter in weight than patio furniture of old, it still has sufficient heft to it and it's completely rust-resistant.

## DRAMATIC PLAY

In the introduction to this chapter, I compared creating a romantic pool to designing a stage set, and the pool shown here is a striking example of theatrical scene-setting at its best.

Situated within the spacious grounds of a Palm Beach estate, the pool area is enclosed on three sides to achieve the intimacy of a dramatic outdoor room. While one side wall is a high hedge sculpted in the shape of undulating waves, the opposite wall is comprised of a raised flower bed. Upstage, and set against a backdrop of towering trees, is a staggered arrangement of stone pedestals supporting a colorful array of greenery and flowering plants, which is echoed in the potted trees and plants arranged like perfectly appointed props along the sides of the pool.

On a patio next to the house, chairs and tables are set up as dining and living room spaces where the owner and his guests can fully appreciate the dramatic setting of the pool.

As variety is the spice of life, it's also the spice of art, so as a contrast to all that lushness and color the patio flooring is a simple arrangement of large stone squares. The chairs and settees are unobtrusive natural wicker, their cushions a solid restful green. It's truly a lesson in the play of point and counterpoint, which is what great theater is all about.

OPPOSITE: In one covered patio area, guests can chat and enjoy drinks and the view of the pool.

ABOVE: Hibiscus blooms add their softness and scent to a tiled dining table.

**ABOVE:** A velvety expanse of grass carpets the backyard of the Spanish-style house.

**LEFT:** At one end of the pool, stately palms provide a verdant backdrop for pedestaled plants.

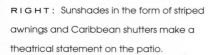

RIGHT: Sunshades in the form of striped awnings and Caribbean shutters make a theatrical statement on the patio.

BELOW: Special effects—both visual and aural—are supplied by water jets spouting from pedestal fountains.

# MODERN ROMANCE

Approaching this southwestern Connecticut property from the Long Island Sound, you immediately see a pair of little square pool houses with rooflines shaped like traditional Chinese hats. Enclosed behind a weathered stone retaining wall (rising more than four feet high where it runs alongside the beach), the property has the vaguely mysterious air of a deserted fort. On the other side of the wall, however, the mood changes completely.

Situated a short distance from the main house, the neat rectangular pool sits like

a tray of blue water on an emerald expanse of lawn. This is romantic style simplified, modernized, and pared down to its stylistic essentials. From this point of view, the pool houses are revealed to be open sun shelters, acting as the casual repositories for an exercise mat, a few fishing poles, and, as occasion demands, wooden steamer chairs that are usually scattered around the patio. The patio is painted to match the seat-wide coping of the pool, and made of practical wooden decking (water simply drains away between the slats). Also, it's confined to only one short side of the pool, which is much more elegant than surrounding it on all four sides.

Romantic touches are made in the form of more subtle nuances: a planter of canna lilies and coleus on a terrace overlooking the pool, and a primitive vine-entwined obelisk.

ABOVE: A view from the lawn encompasses distant boats on the Sound and generous helpings of sky.

OPPOSITE: Classic steamer chairs of natural wood blend into their subtly colored surroundings.

**ABOVE:** Situated a short distance from the house, the pool is accessed via a quick walk across the lawn.

**LEFT:** Here, the romantic vision is simple, elegant, and brilliantly designed for its setting.

**LEFT:** A pot garden of canna lilies and coleus sits on a railed terrace overlooking the Sound.

**RIGHT:** When the fish are biting, rods are at the ready on one of the peak-roofed follies.

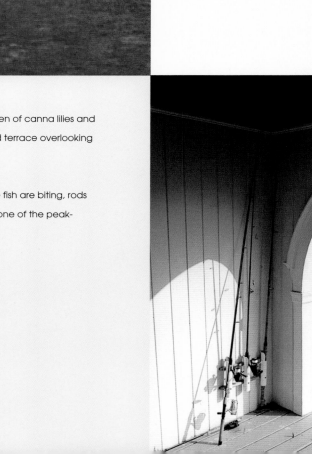

ABOVE: Beachside, the stone enclosure wall rises a good 4 feet from the ground.

LEFT: A circular opening built into the stone wall will soon contain a minigarden of plants.

# CLASSICALLY ROMANTIC

On another Hamptons property, landscape architect Christopher LaGuardia drew from a number of style sources to compose this impressive interpretation of romantic.

Its showpiece, for example, is a modern pool made up of an assembly of rectangles. The squared-off water spouts on its raised side walls are updated takes on primitive clay conduits that you can still find in parts of old-world Europe. The sharply rectangular basins that compose the nearby spa (located just off of a terrace that leads to the house) are also clearly modern in design.

Plant materials cascading into the water soften the lines of the pool. At one end, an upstanding trio of Greek columns suggests the classic and the romantic. Finally, there are the lavish plantings of trees and shrubs that edge right up to one of the pool's jigsawed sides to create a natural juxtaposition of trees and water that's nothing short of rustic.

Considered from a practical perspective, the entire pool area is a successful marriage of form and function. Measuring 90 by 30 feet at its longest and widest, the pool is large enough to comfortably accommodate a crowd when the owners entertain. The cushioned chaises made of lightweight plastic can be easily moved to the surrounding lawn or repositioned anywhere along the wide swath of coping.

From a purely aesthetic view, the entire mix makes for an enticingly romantic setting that surpasses the sum of its parts.

OPPOSITE: Cascades spouting from squares of stone create water music and rippled light.

ABOVE: At one pool corner, Grecian columns in a woodsy setting recall romantic glories of the past.

## SPAS AND HOT TUBS

The ancient world was well aware of the health benefits and calming effects induced by soaking in heated water, and the earliest known proof of this knowledge can be found at the Stabian baths in Pompeii. Built by the Romans in the second century BC, this public bathing facility featured an alveus, or a hot bath heated by a hypocaust that circulated hot air through a series of flues hidden behind the room's walls and beneath its mosaic-tiled floor. In effect, this comparatively simple yet impressively efficient contrivance was the early precursor to our modern hot tub (or what in swimming-pool circles is often referred to as a spa). In its twenty-first century translation, the hot-bath room has been reduced to the size of a large tub, typically a shallow minipool with built-in seating, and often equipped with amenities that the early Romans would have envied.

Among them: an adjustable temperature control (usually set between 80 and 90 degrees Fahrenheit) and pulsating water jets (also adjustable) that do wonders for soothing tired muscles and persuading tangled nerves to unravel and relax.

For many pool owners, a spa is the perfect setting for enjoying a relaxing drink with friends, as well as a safe place for young children to enjoy the heated water while sitting

on a parent's lap. Also, if your pool is not heated, a soak in the spa will warm your blood before or after a bracing swim.

While all hot tubs are referred to as spas, not all spas are hot tubs. In some situations, for example, one end-section of a swimming pool may be walled in to create a smaller pool-within-a-pool. Such minipools are often reserved for the Water Wings set who are just learning to swim; or, if provided with seating, for those adults who just want to rest, cool off, and chat without having to get completely wet.

A spa may be round or oval, square or rectangular, or even some geometrical amalgam of these forms. The shape of the spa or hot tub is used to complement the pool, either repeating the rectangular lines or providing a contrasting circular design. Sometimes the spa is tucked off to the side with adjoining plant materials for privacy and another form of ornament. On the other hand, it can be placed front and center and used as a focal point for the pool area.

The placement of a spa will vary as well. It might be sunken into a pool's patio paving, perched on top of it, or designed to project right into the body of the pool. In whatever guise, a spa can turn out to be your pool's most popular accessory.

# OASIS IN MARRAKECH

Not long ago, while traveling through Morocco, I discovered a fascinating little inn just outside the city of Marrakech. Originally an old casbah (the Arab word for fortress), the Tigmi, as it's called, was converted and is now run by owner Max Lawrence, who graciously gave me a guided tour.

Though the hotel is relatively small, it has a sprawling layout. After climbing up and down various staircases and following a maze of intriguing little corridors, we emerged into the outer environs with its interconnected courtyards. At the centerpiece of one of these enclosures is a pool, the color of its water shining like a jewel in its neutral-toned surroundings. Constructed of cement and polished limestone, the pool has coping of the same materials mixed with a yellow marble powder that makes it skid-free. And at one end, it has a small L-shaped extension with underwater benches built into the walls, an area referred to as a "salon corner," where people can comfortably meet and talk without obstructing lap swimmers.

Like the wooden furnishings and decorative elements (a sculptural stand of cedars, several large earthen jars positioned on small beds of pebbles), the pool design is faithfully authentic to its locale. Lawrence explained that he wanted to build a very simple water presence to fit with the earthen feel of the house.

However, his favorite aspect of this romantic desert oasis is the poolside view over the Haouz Plain to the distant High Atlas Mountains.

ABOVE: A covered patio and an open lawn cater to shade- and sun-lovers respectively.

OPPOSITE: On a windless day, the water mirrors weathered walls, spiky trees, and candles floating in the pool.

ABOVE: The Tigmi pool and sand-hued patio look as timeless as the land around it.

RIGHT: Sling chairs and a handy table provide the necessary comforts on a poolside platform.

LEFT: At night, half-globe candles glow on the pool's surface like floating points of starlight.

**LEFT:** Drainage stones under a clay jar help maintain the plant's optimum moisture level.

**BELOW:** Cushioned daybeds beneath a portico invite relaxed conversation in shaded comfort.

**ABOVE:** An open, log-roofed passage leads to the hotel bedrooms.

**BELOW:** A wall-sided walkway lined with cypress trees suggests the parapet of an ancient castle.

# NEW ENGLAND IN AMAGANSETT

Each landscaping job has its own set of challenges, and the pool area I designed for a 1970s-era house in Amagansett, New York, was no exception. A year earlier, I'd been commissioned to rework the rest of the property in an old-fashioned romantic style I refer to as "Nantucket cottage," and when the owners decided to renovate their pool, they wanted to mimic that style.

When they initially planned to install a pool and realized that their long, narrow lot couldn't accommodate one, they bought an adjacent (and similar-sized) lot—which happened to be a good 8 feet higher! To join the two grades, I used stone walls to carve out a series of flagstoned terraces.

Encouraged by the architectural elements introduced with these levels, I then envisioned chaises on a raised patio platform overlooking the pool. Not only did the finished platform add another element to the flat horizontal of the pool, but it also made the pool look larger than it actually was.

The two-room pool house, attached to the back of the newly built garage, had one room outfitted as a kitchen and the other as a changing room. The architect's idea of adding a mirrored wall to each room was a great visual ploy that created the illusion of enlarged rooms and connected them to the pergola-shaded patio and pool just outside the doors.

The finishing touches: the old-boat look of mahogany stain on the pool house's wooden shingles and pergola, and the lashings of flowers that typify the most traditional of New England's seaside cottages—which was just what the owners had in mind.

OPPOSITE: Pool water laps against the front "porch" of a two-room shelter with mirrored back walls.

ABOVE: In a pergola-covered dining area, twin columns support the stone top of a table.

**LEFT:** Hydrangeas and other graceful flowers tumble along the borders of a multilevel walkway.

**BELOW:** Striped chaise cushions and stiff-postured umbrellas add distinction to the raised-platform patio.

LEFT: Umbrellas provide shelter from the sun, but at certain times of day the nearby trees serve the same function and provide dappled shade over the water.

RIGHT: Lush greenery and stone-slab steps define a romantic stairway leading down from road to pool.

BELOW: Stylish wooden grids provide an entrance gate and protective fencing for part of the pool area.

# A JAMAICAN SAMPLER

Like all professional landscapers, I'm always on the lookout for good ideas, and at the resort club of Round Hill in Jamaica I found a treasure trove of them. Dotted over the hillside facing a fabulous view of Montego Bay, the privately owned houses and pools, as well as the clubhouse, the club dining room, and the tennis courts,

have all been designed with luxury in mind. In addition to its own pool, each house has a private outdoor dining room that's both elegant and intimate. Poolside furniture might include a canopied double bed (which, with the addition of swaths of netting, I could easily envision sleeping in under the stars).

Round Hill isn't a brand-spanking-new development, but a decades-old establishment, which means that all of the stonework has achieved the inimitable weathered patina of age, and the palms, bougainvillea, and other tropical plants framing scenes of the bay are in the full glory of their maturity.

Each element is lovely and beautifully maintained, and certain special touches are particularly eye-catching, such as the oval glass top of a patio dining table that seems to float within its enclosure of bamboo Chippendale-style chairs, the collection of bleached conch shells displayed atop the stone wall of a garden bed, and the white Adirondack-inspired chairs on the clubhouse porch. Look for yourself and you're sure to find inspirations for your own personal ideas of luxury.

ABOVE: Geraniums in weathered stone pots beautify a corner of a pool patio.

OPPOSITE: For serious lounging, patio furnishings include the luxury of a canopied bed—mattresses, bolsters, and all.

ABOVE: In the foreground, a delicate branch of bougainvillea seems to float on the surface of the pool.

RIGHT: As daylight fades, a small elongated pool captures the image of a palm growing on the hillside.

LEFT: In Round Hill, flowers spilling over a wall are standard decoration for an outdoor dining room.

**LEFT:** In one Round Hill house, Chinese Chippendale-style dining chairs add a note of formality to the tropical ambiance.

**BELOW:** Almost everywhere you look, nature seems to provide a painted backdrop for the scene before it.

**ABOVE:** From high atop a Jamaican hill, a poolside view includes the waters of Montego Bay.

**BELOW:** Comfy seating and outdoor views make the clubhouse veranda a popular spot for cocktails.

MODERN

# THE MODERN POOL

"Less is more." That well-known phrase from Bauhaus architect Ludwig Mies van der Rohe sums up the essence of the pure, clean, uncluttered look of modern style. Shapes are boldly geometric.

Colors are neutral. Accessories are kept to an absolute minimum. Sometimes modern renderings are merely skeletal suggestions of traditional forms from the past; sometimes they break with tradition entirely to forge fresh new statements of their own.

Whatever the interpretation, the word *sculptural* is always key. That is, without the distraction of extraneous adornments, each modern piece—a chaise, a table, even a pool rail—stands out as a bold, artistic declaration and thereby achieves heightened importance. The absence of decoration puts a greater emphasis on the use of space and proportion (for example, by juxtaposing the contrast of vertical and horizontal surfaces) to achieve the desired effect, which is, paradoxically, both dramatic and soothingly tranquil.

ABOVE: This sleek, elegant tiled spa epitomizes modern style.

OPPOSITE: Sail-shaped tarps shade the wooden-decked landing of a modern pool on Pointe Milou.

# POOL ON THE PRAIRIE

One test to measure the validity of an architectural design is to see how naturally it fits into its surroundings. Another is to see how effectively its horizontal and vertical elements play against one another. The Long Island, New York, house and pool area shown here earns top marks on both counts.

Given the interesting, almost prairielike expanse of land enclosing this Amagansett property, the owner had clear ideas about how he wanted the new construction to look. The result is a modern mix of new tech and Old West that sits so comfortably in the landscape as to seem a natural component of it. The L-shaped

house, a wood and glass sculpture made up of geometric boxes, serves as a striking vertical contrast to the horizontal patio decking and long, narrow pool with its smaller reflecting pool positioned below it like the dot of an exclamation point.

The most intriguing feature is the sail-like canvas wall running along one of the pool area's long sides. Suspended from the top bar of an open wooden frame, the sails, when secured to the bottom rod, become a privacy wall and windbreak so that with every strong breeze they billow like the canvas sides of an old prairie schooner. When freed, they flap like freshly laundered sheets on a clothesline, flooding the pool area with brilliant light and unveiling spectacular sunset views.

OPPOSITE: On a prairielike parcel of Amagansett, billowing canvas and a pool's reflection work modern magic.

ABOVE: With canvas untied and flying free, the side wall opens the pool to ocean breezes.

**ABOVE:** The streamlined design of the wheeled chaises is as spare and unfussy as the surroundings.

**BELOW:** One section of the house has rolling wooden panels that cover—or expose—sliding glass doors.

**ABOVE:** The pool shape is an exclamation point whose bottom square is furnished for in-water lounging.

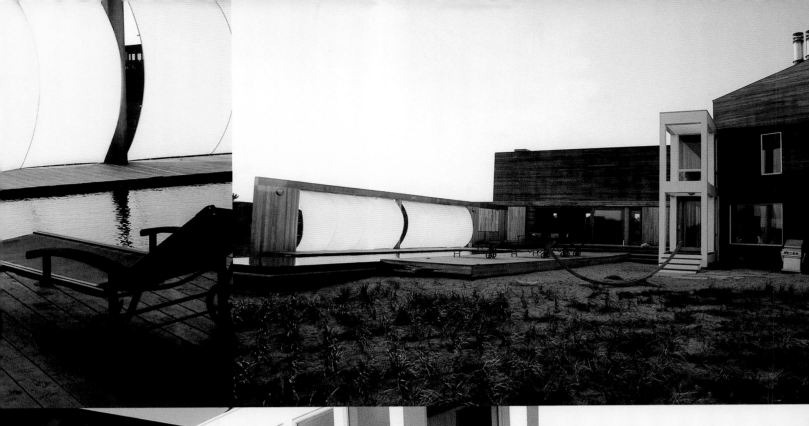

**ABOVE:** The L-shaped house and canvas wall form a tightly integrated unit around the pool.

**LEFT:** A nice touch: The upper frames of a multiwindowed wall echo the shape of the pool.

**ABOVE:** With this infinity pool style, an outer wall receives and recycles water pouring over the pool's sides.

**LEFT:** Before and after dips, an outdoor shower becomes a luxurious convenience.

**OPPOSITE, ABOVE:** For this pool style, wire fencing—fully exposed and sans plant cover—was a perfect choice.

**OPPOSITE, BELOW:** An arrangement of seashells makes a sculptural statement on a corner of the deck.

# ISLAND PARADISE

At the end of a remote, windswept peninsula on the French West Indies island of St. Barts is a little piece of blue heaven. Shutters, doors, walkways, pool water—just about everything here is colored in soft shades of turquoise blue that somehow manage to mimic the surrounding sea and sky, whatever the time of day.

The tile-edged pool is sleek and modern. The main area is made for lap swimming; its little offshoot a perfect alcove for resting your folded arms on the pool's edge while taking in the spectacular scenery spread out before you.

One section of the pool shares a wall with a garden bed that gently slopes down from a raised terrace, and beneath another part of the terrace is a trough that releases a cascade of water into the pool with the flip of a switch.

The house is designed to accommodate its setting—which means that, in true island fashion, it's quite long and only one room deep, with plenty of doors and windows along the front and back walls so that the chambers in between become virtual breezeways. It's the kind of setup that makes a pool house superfluous and entertaining effortless.

In a setting like this, with its theatrical changes of light and nonstop sky show of clouds, little more is needed in the way of ornament than, say, a painted vase for adding some decorative interest to a clean white wall, the fascinating shapes of a few poolside plants making a pleasant contrast against the water, and for music, some snapping flags catching the rhythms of the wind.

ABOVE: Beyond the blue doors, the sea, the pool, and gracious island living await.

OPPOSITE: With the turn of a gizmo, a waterfall pours from the roof and plunges into the pool.

**ABOVE:** Patterns on a lovely ceramic vase punctuate the white-and-turquoise color scheme.

**BELOW:** A giant agave plant is just one of the gray-blue-shaded varieties of plants around the pool.

**ABOVE:** Cream-colored blooms peek over edge of the pool's shimmering blue water.

**RIGHT:** The vertical element of these plants plays against the horizontal landscape beyond.

**A B O V E :** One section of the terraced garden slopes past the pool and downward to the sea.

**L E F T :** No matter what time of day, the color of this pool water matches that of the ocean. In the morning, it's a gorgeous shade of azure blue, while in the evening it becomes a moody gray.

**B E L O W :** An international assembly of flags stands tall before the early-morning sky.

## MODERN MEDITERRANEAN

Venice, the city of canals, might well have been the conceptual springboard for this modern pool on Florida's eastern coast. Located in the resort community of Windsor, just north of Vero Beach, it was designed by Hugh Jacobsen, whose idea of abutting the pool against the house absolutely delights the owners' grandkids. The reason: The house's windows open onto the pool, so swimmers can jump from the living room right into the water.

Look closely and you'll find other old-world hints as well—the proliferation of weathered shutters that flank the floor-to-ceiling windows, for example, the wealth of porous travertine marble patio, and the open porch areas. This modern version of Mediterranean style is distilled to its essence so that familiar utilitarian elements such as the square-shaped metal railings for the pool and spa and the poolside chaises and tables are virtual works of art in themselves. Delightful bronze renditions of a bear cub and an alligator by furniture sculptor/designer Judy McKie offer art that doubles as seating.

But what the owners particularly love about this lovely square-shaped pool is the way the dark water reflects the shutter-windowed wall of the house. And possibly, with its infinity edge looking out on the view of a little canal, a rolling golf course, and a limitless stretch of sky, this pool is capable of stirring reflections of a different kind as well.

OPPOSITE: Square-paned windows—a modern take on European tradition—push upward for indoor access to the pool.

ABOVE: A winding canal separates the infinity pool from the golf course across the way.

**ABOVE:** Metal fish form the back-rests of chairs on a dining patio near the pool.

**LEFT:** A bronze alligator resides on a strip of lawn between the infinity pool and the canal.

**LEFT:** Trained vines, a tall shutter, and an elegant little bistro chair evoke the essence of a Mediterranean courtyard.

**RIGHT:** Here, the old-world style windowpanes are repeated in the steel squares of a modern handrail.

**ABOVE**: Hugh Jacobsen's sleek chaises and a circular spa serve to break up the white expanse of the travertine paving.

**LEFT**: Furnishings in an open-air living room blend the best design elements of old and new.

**ABOVE:** Tucked to one side, a small roofed structure discreetly houses mechanical workings for the pool.

**RIGHT:** The friendly alligator seat is a piece of bronze artwork by sculptor/designer Judy McKie.

**BELOW:** A pebble-paved glade provides sanctuary for a modern birdbath.

**LEFT:** In subtropical Florida, Caribbean-style shutters filter sunlight without blocking welcome breezes.

**OPPOSITE:** A polished railing reflects dark pool water on one surface, light marble paving on another.

# CLASSICALLY MODERN

During the Hamptons building boom that began erupting in the 1970s, longtime residents peering from the windows of their traditional resort houses were often confounded by the glass, wood, and steel structures that were mushrooming up all around them. Many of these modern homes—including the main house of this Bridgehampton property—were the brain children of the late visionary modernist Norman Jaffe.

Not long ago, when the present owner wanted to build a pool area, he called in architect Christopher LaGuardia to design one that would be in sync with the style

of the house Jaffe designed. The impressive result is the pool you see here.

Because the land sloped down from the house to the pool site, LaGuardia connected the two levels with wide-stepped dining and lounging terraces. Together, the cascading corners of the terrace stairs paved by buff-toned stone create a sense of spaciousness, which, for all its simplicity, is loaded with a structural interest that has the capacity to turn sunlight and shadow into ever-changing pieces of art. What's more, it instills the grandeur more commonly associated with the kind of great plazas surrounding classical civic buildings.

By way of landscaping, the far side of the L-shaped pool abuts an apron of lawn surrounded by sheltering bushes and trees. Some of my favorite touches are the collection of sculptural amelanchier trees undulating upward from square beds of shaggy liriope; the shocks of sea grass sprouting from big earthenware bowls arranged along the edge of a terrace; and, reclining on the lawn, a totally outrageous life-sized cow sculpture in bold colors. (Somehow, I think Jaffe would have liked it, too.)

ABOVE: The simple curve of an earthen bowl makes a perfect foil for unruly strands of seagrass inside it.

OPPOSITE: Waterspouts line a projecting platform furnished with a neat row of chaises.

**ABOVE:** Pool equipment finds an unobtrusive spot in a slope of lawn behind a tapering stone wall.

**LEFT:** Next to the dining terrace, amelanchier trees rise from beds of grassy liriope.

**BELOW LEFT:** Style-defining details: green glass tiles embedded along the waterline beneath putty-knifed coping.

**BELOW:** A bowl of sea grass makes a statement on a terrace above the pool.

**ABOVE:** Multilevel terraces surrounding the pool each serve their own purpose, whether for lounging, dining, or as a spot to enjoy the wonderful view.

**RIGHT:** On a brighter side (literally) is a life-sized cow painted all the colors of the rainbow.

# GATES, WALLS, AND FENCES

Gates, walls, and fences, more than any other elements, will probably be determined by your pool code. The standard rule for structures enclosing the pool area is that they must be at least 4 feet high. Within these code parameters, however, there are many attractive ways to make a virtue of necessity so that these safety barriers can be a positive asset to the overall pool design. When choosing a gate, always keep that vision in mind,

then feel free to experiment with shapes, styles, colors, and materials that will best work within it. You have the options of matching the gate to the walls or fences that flank it, or of choosing one that offers an unexpected contrast to them, like the delicacy of antique ironwork placed against overscaled stone walls. Although 4 feet is the minimum required height, extending the height may actually prove to be more aesthetically pleasing.

For example, imagine a beautiful, out-sized antique door incorporated into a high stucco wall or a yew-hedge fence. Your gate might be a classic wooden picket, a double-latticed door, a wooden grid, or a piece of exquisite ironwork. Open-worked gates like these also have the advantage of admitting light, which can visually soften the rigidity of a solid wall or hedge.

For fencing, you could opt for standard

wooden pickets, simple metal bars, or decorative ironwork. Or you could go with a utilitarian cyclone or other heavy-gage wire fence that can be camouflaged with vines or hidden behind hedges.

But aside from satisfying code requirements, walls and fences (which include railings) serve other functions that might be classified as practical, aesthetic, or both. For example, every pool needs boundaries of some kind, some clearly visible delineation that establishes its limits—and marks its importance—within the property (or that actually serves to separate the area from a neighbor's property). That same idea may extend to raised terraces and patios, where decorative iron railings, or perhaps a stone balustrade, will not only establish boundaries for those spaces, but also give them authority and, in some cases, provide a necessary safety barrier to guard against falls. And in the case of pool-area gardens, protective fencing will often be needed to discourage foraging rabbits and the ever-increasing population of deer. Finally, when they're high enough, certain types of fences (like basket-weaves, pickets, trellises, and so on), as well as walls of brick, stucco, or stone, can provide the privacy that many pool owners consider essential.

# STEPPING-STONE POOL

Set apart from the other dwellings that comprise the private resort community of Round Hill, Jamaica, is an Asian-inspired house and pool that are as breathtaking as the Montego Bay view that surrounds them. This isn't the first instance of Far

Eastern elements melding with modern Western style; nor, given the compatibility of this pared-down approach to design, will it be the last.

Before one enters the courtyard, a swath of shallow water rimmed with a primitive rock garden and intriguing thatch-roofed lighting fixtures gives a hint of what lies within. Beyond the gateway and central courtyard are stepping-stones that seem to float on the aquamarine pool.

Describing the pool's shape as free-form would not do it justice. Beginning simply as a tiny, elongated lagoon in front of one of the two houses, it morphs into a perfectly geometric swimming pool with fixed stepping-stones, then widens to become an infinity-edged pond where a roofed dining platform juts out into it like an elegant peninsula.

One of the great things about modern style is how easily it accepts sculptural elements from what may appear to be radically different sources. In this case, that means exotic artifacts such as a copper elephant and intricately carved gateway doors, resulting in a mix of ancient and modern that comprises timelessness.

OPPOSITE: Hints of Asia inform the architecture of structures embracing a paved courtyard and its stepping-stone pool.

ABOVE: The small ears of this weathered copper elephant suggest an Indian or East Asian origin.

**OPPOSITE:** A fully articulated multi-peaked roof rests on four pillars of a dining platform projecting into the pool.

**CENTER ABOVE:** A whimsical metal cat holds a shallow dish (to attract thirsty birds on a rainy day perhaps?).

**CENTER BELOW:** On one of several connected pool areas, more stones form a path to the pool's infinity edge.

**ABOVE:** The pool's stationary stones can be used as a pathway—or as convenient tables for resting drinks upon.

**LEFT:** Dendrobium orchids add a change of color to the corner of a lounging terrace.

# MINIMALISM AT ITS FINEST

On the French West Indies island of St. Barts, hillside properties like this one must have been the setting that designers had in mind when they came up with the idea of infinity pools. The example shown here looks out over the lush tropical landscape

onto Pointe Milou so that when the owners, John and Frances Bowes, swim morning laps, it isn't hard for them to imagine that the pool and sea have magically melded into a single body of water.

If ever a pool could be described as minimalistic modern, this one would be it. The furnishings are uncluttered and sleek; the color scheme, a simple palette of white against blue water and natural wood. The aesthetic appeal of the pool patio's simple design has practical advantages as well. For example, the weathered teakwood decking surrounding the pool is easily maintained and cooler on the feet because its light, sun-bleached color is less prone to absorb heat, even in direct sunlight.

The furnishings are another case in point. In the shaded living/dining area, the outsized sectional sofa is fashioned from canvas cushions on a simple teakwood base. Lined in a series along one side of the pool, the chaises are mesh-bodied with cast-aluminum frames so that cleaning is just a matter of spraying them with a hose.

No single element is extraneous. Here the bare-bones simplicity of the man-made setting serves to complement the natural one that surrounds it—which, given the surroundings in question, is just as it should be.

ABOVE: Fate candles in ceramic holders add a warm glow to relaxed gatherings under the stars.

OPPOSITE: Shaded seating is positioned for overlooking the pool and the coral islands that pattern St. Barts' surrounding waters.

**LEFT:** Gorgeous blooms add a note of primitive beauty to the clean-lined furnishings of a dining area.

**LEFT:** From this deck side view, palm tree tops can be seen waving above the lap pool's edge.

**RIGHT:** For cooling off, there are out-sized sunshades and chaises made of breeze-catching aluminum mesh.

**ABOVE LEFT:** When the canvas panels behind the banquette are lifted, loungers are treated to a spectacular 360-degree view.

**ABOVE:** In another dining spot, rattan armchairs look as impressive as the ceramic twig candlesticks on the table.

**LEFT:** Seen up close, the sculptural construction of a chaise makes a design statement all by itself.

# SCULPTURES AND ORNAMENTS

Regardless of its style or shape, your basic swimming pool is simply a large horizontal plane—an expanse that could be visually uninteresting without vertical elements to balance it. Ornaments and sculptural pieces not only supply that element, but they also help to inform the pool area with your own personal taste and sense of style. What's more, thoughtfully chosen additions can go

a long way toward authenticating the style of the pool area itself.

"Sculpture" is a category that covers a wide range of options. It might mean an original artwork of great value or an affordable reproduction. It could be an architectural artifact that's in mint condition or a time-battered remnant of one with power to stir the mind with musings about its once-glorious

past. A sculpture might also refer to a classic or romantic representation of the human form, of flowers or fruit in an urn, or simply of the urn itself. It could depict a single animal, or several animals in a group. It might even depict a mythical grotesque. Aside from its subject matter, the material and size of a sculpture present further choices. It might be made of bronze, stone, wood, or other

weatherproof material. It can be gargantuan or life-sized or small. For maximum impact, you should place a piece as carefully as you choose it. For example, original large-scale sculptures, especially those of museum quality, should be displayed at judiciously chosen spots on the patio to show them off to best advantage. Antique stone garden ornaments can be placed at the corners of a pool to define its boundaries and make it seem more intimate, or they can flank a gate to the pool area, designating it as the main entry to the pool.

Less costly alternatives can be equally effective. One of my favorites is metal balls that float in the pool, continually changing like spherical kaleidoscopes as they reflect water, light, sky, and scenery on their shiny curved surfaces. Flags are colorful adornments that add movement and sound to the scene as they snap and billow with each passing breeze. Ornaments and sculptures can punctuate a pool style with drama, romance, color, and whimsy.

# POOL WITH A VIEW

Embracing the curve of the state's southern coast, the Florida Keys are spread out like a string of beads between the turquoise waters of the Florida Bay and the Straits of Florida. Given the scenic splendors and tropical climate, without a doubt this is serious pool territory—as shown by the shining example featured here.

Situated on the low-lying island of Key Largo, this modern pool is a stylistic amalgam. On its landward side, the free-form shape conforms to the flowing contours of an expansive flagstone patio, while the opposite side is infinity-edged to incorporate the endless view. But where most infinity pools have a color-tinted lining to match the water they overlook, this one achieves the same effect with ceramic tiles in a palette ranging from the lightest blue to the deepest royal. When seen from a distance, the colors meld together so that the pool and its spa seem like natural extensions of water and sky.

In keeping with the dictates of true modern style, plants are nonexistent and all other decorative additions are kept to an absolute minimum. To accommodate seating, there's a cushioned banquette snuggled into an arc of the coral stone wall. Special touches include a pair of ceramic pots, a simple jade-leaf design on the ironwork detail flanking the banquette, and the vertical arc of a dolphin set beneath the overhang of the house, which offers a shady respite from the tropical sun.

OPPOSITE: Underwater steps next to a tapering curved wall lead into the depths of the pool.

ABOVE: A cushioned banquette fits snugly into a contoured wall that was custom-built for it.

**ABOVE:** The pleasing convex line of a dolphin sculpture frames a pool-and-sea view from the patio.

**RIGHT:** The free-form pool includes a curved infinity edge overlooking trees and distant water.

**BELOW:** Branches of jade are beautifully captured in this metal insert in a boundary wall.

**R I G H T :** Like impressionist art, the multihued mosaic of the pool tiles merges with the color of the sea.

**B E L O W :** An appealing ceramic fish makes a colorful splash against the neutral stonework of the patio.

# A POSH TAKE ON HIGH-TECH

With two chalk-white Philippe Starck club chairs sharply contrasted against the blue-black stone floor of the forecourt, the spare modernism of this East Hampton, New York, pool area is well-established even before you pass through the wooden grill entry gate.

Along the path to the pool, high-tech portholes embedded in the paving's edge act as guide lights for evening swims, while tall, fence-backed hedges offer privacy

for the pool and patio they enclose. Within this clean, uncluttered enclosure, every element has a sculptural significance. For example, the simple oblong pool sports a curved arch of steel that serves as a railing for steps separating a shallow section of the pool (which is great for toddlers) from the deeper water used by adults.

Along each of the pool's long sides, a patio of stone squares set within wide grids of cement provides lounge space for chaises. The cushioned teak chaises recall the distinctive lines of classic Danish modern style.

In another part of the pool area, there's an example of a very neat (in both senses of the word) landscaping idea for settings like this one. Encircling a patriarchal tree, the same dark stones seen in the forecourt serve as a garden bed for spherical green shrubs that seem to sprout from it like a bevy of whimsical pom-pons.

ABOVE: At the pool's shallow end, access steps are accommodated by a curved steel handrail.

OPPOSITE: Chaises that hark back to Danish modern furnish a stone-and-ceramic grid patio.

**ABOVE:** Rather than wrapping around the pool, the concrete and bluestone patio is extended on either side to accommodate areas for chaises.

**FAR LEFT:** Metal-framed porthole lamps are a nice high-tech solution for lighting a paved walkway.

**LEFT:** The paving, chairs, and simple grid gate are a foretaste of stylistic tech treats to come.

**RIGHT:** Shrub globes in an ebon bed offer a good example of pared-down, modern garden style.

# NEW LOOK AT NANTUCKET TRADITION

The Massachusetts island of Nantucket is famous for its charming old seaside houses and country cottages. Since the islanders have the good sense to revere their architectural treasures, all new construction must conform to very strict codes that preserve the area's integrity. The property you see here—a pool and a single house designed to look like a cluster of cottages—is a modern take on Nantucket tradition.

Located in the community of Siasconset, it was created by architect Hugh Jacobsen. His clients, the heads of a large family, wanted a simple, low-maintenance house and pool area to use as their own private residence (an addendum to three older structures elsewhere on the property used as guesthouses for the owner's children).

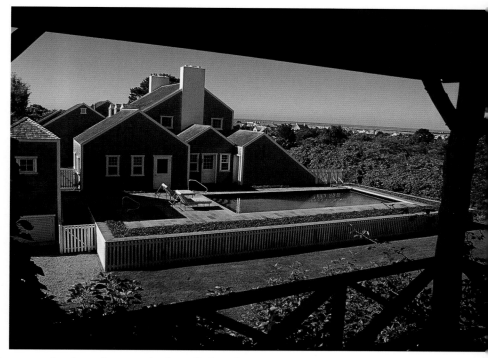

The pool area and furnishings Jacobsen designed suited their needs to a T. The pool is a clean rectangle raised the requisite 4 feet above ground level for safety purposes and contained on three sides by a concrete wall. In true island spirit, the wall's facade is a sleek version of a classic picket fence. For continuity, the verticals of the fence are repeated on the backings of the handsome chaises; their tube-metal construction is in turn echoed by the flowing shapes of the pool's access ladder railings.

The foliage is just as minimal. There are no garden beds or potted plants to tend to; a vinca ground cover frames the pool, and of course there is the beautiful blue backdrop that nature provides free of charge.

OPPOSITE: A tech-look picket fence—a concession to Nantucket tradition—cleverly masks the pool area's boundary wall.

ABOVE: The cluster of salt-box-inspired cottages are conjoined to function as a single house.

# OUTDOOR DINING

Though I've never been able to answer the "why" of it to my complete satisfaction, it's a known fact that food always tastes better outdoors. The French term for it is eating *en plein air*, so there's a suggestion that fresh air has something to do with the phenomenon. Our own closest equivalent is "picnicking" which, for me at least, harks back to that childhood sense of delight that comes with engaging in a commonplace activity (eating a meal) in untraditional surroundings (not the indoor dining room). But whatever we call it, the instantaneous associations engendered by the idea of eating outdoors are always pleasurable ones. (Remember that joyous painterly description of Renoir's, *The Luncheon of the Boating Party*? One look and you know that all those people under the fluttering red-and-white canopy are having a terrific time. Even the little dog seems to be smiling!) When outdoor dining means poolside dining—which may include anything from a juice and corn-flakes breakfast, to an impromptu afternoon barbecue, to an elaborate dinner party under the stars—the pleasure can be even greater because, to a large extent, you get to determine the fine points of what the *en plein air* experience will be like. For example, you may want to site the patio's dining area beneath the dappled shade of a vine-

covered pergola that looks out on a view of the pool and garden. Or create a dining space within the elegant column supports of a loggia. A Moroccan tent, an open-sided shelter, or even a walled shelter with an uncovered pergola roof offer still more options. As for furnishing your chosen space, nowadays you can choose from a wonderful selection of outdoor dining tables and chairs in just about any style. Modern furniture may

be simple, hard-edged, or even avant-garde renditions that are pieces of art in themselves. For romantic or classic settings there's a whole range of traditional styles to choose from. If your pool is rustic, you might opt for bistro chairs, or the type of simple, countrified pieces you'd expect to find in a farmhouse kitchen. Your best bets are solid, weatherproof pieces that you can cover and keep on the patio year-round without worrying

about winter storage. Another good tip is to look for tables that are large enough to seat a crowd when entertaining.

As for cookers, you're no doubt aware that the latest outdoor grills are stainless steel and state-of-the-art. They're also designed to fit into any number of outdoor settings, from the minikitchen of a pool house to a simple flat-topped wall used to define the dining area of a patio.

# CLASSIC

# THE CLASSIC POOL

A classically styled pool setting can be gauged by weighing in on four elements: order, restraint, symmetry, and balance. Typically, if the pool is sited next to or within immediate view of the house, it will be perfectly parallel or exactly perpendicular to it. Quite often the house, pool, and patio area are each on a different level so that when you move from one to the other you feel as though you're passing through different rooms.

In deference to balance and symmetry, access stairs are often sited at each end of the pool's cross axis, perhaps with a fountain placed at the axes' meeting point.

For this setting, furniture is minimalist in style, and plants—whether manicured or natural—are suggestive of a classic tradition from the past.

Finally, to all the above indications of classic style, I'd venture to add the word *elegance*—and when you see the pools shown on the following pages, you'll readily understand why.

ABOVE: Alongside the pool, striped chaises sport little white towels embroidered with starfish.

OPPOSITE: The materials of this pool and spa— steel, mahogany, and limestone—epitomize sleek classic style.

# A TROPICAL CLASSIC

We so often equate classic style with ancient Greece that we sometimes forget there are many other styles within that larger category. Tropical classic, as exemplified by the beautiful pool shown here, is one of them.

Built in the 1940s as part of an estate in southeastern Florida, the pool area is enclosed in its own private enclave: next to the ocean but protected from it, near

the main house but not overshadowed by it. From the uppermost terrace just outside the house, you descend to another terrace and a double-winged staircase with weathered stone balusters, and then down a single flight of steps to the level of the ovate pool.

The surrounding cement patio runs right up to the pool's edge, but even without coping, its borders are delineated by a continuous strip of blue-and-white mosaic tiles running along the top edge of the pool walls.

Just off the patio is a loggialike structure with a peaked wooden roof. One end of this shelter is furnished as a living room; the other is comfortably set up for dining.

Everywhere you look, tropical flowers and plants burgeon from garden beds, spill over walls, and shoot up like leafy umbrellas making music in the wind and filling the air with their exotic perfumes.

ABOVE: Stairs cut into notched-out corners are simple and elegant, while luscious plant materials soften the look of the poolside balustrade.

OPPOSITE: Old-fashioned, oversized bamboo chairs epitomize poolside comfort and relaxation.

ABOVE: The purple-netted petals of a cymbidium orchid beautify the corner of a covered seating area.

BELOW: A classic, beautiful balustrade satisfies the code for pool fencing.

ABOVE: Within the loggialike setting of the pretty living room area, color and comfort are key.

LEFT: Cobalt chairs, ceramic vases, and a sextet of fish add punches of color to a neutral-walled dining area.

**ABOVE:** From this sunny-walled terrace, twin stairways lead to the pool area and surrounding patio.

**LEFT:** Delightful wall fountains like this one are familiar accessories in classic garden design.

**BELOW:** Wonderful cushion fabric and embroidered towels add a stylish touch to these chaises.

## SLEEK BEAUTY

Celebrated fashion designer and interior design book author Carolyne Roehm's innate good taste guaranteed success when she created this lovely pool enclosure on her property in northwestern Connecticut.

Viewed as a whole, the effect is unmistakably classic (ordered, balanced, and refined). But with a closer look at individual details of that picture, it becomes clear that the materials themselves borrow from both rustic and romantic styles. For example, plantings of willows and other old-growth trees become a romantic frame for the classically rectangular pool. On the patio, supporting a lineup of green-and-

white striped chaises, earthy bricks are arranged in a formal herringbone pattern. Behind the patio, draperies of lush wisteria shade a pergola's trellised roof, and beneath that bit of romance is the traditional look of two Chippendale-style garden benches, which, like all the wood furnishings, are painted a classic dark green.

In keeping with the pervading color scheme, all of the flowers—from the iceberg roses in their terra-cotta pots to the clematis on the wooden obelisks—are white. Also worth noting is the fact that the furnishing elements are deliberately oversized in proportion with the large area they inhabit.

Carolyne Roehm loves entertaining luncheon guests in the shelter, even though it's some distance from the house and isn't equipped with a kitchen. Her creative solution: prepare all the food ahead of time and then have it transported from the main house to the shelter on a golf cart.

OPPOSITE: In this classically formal pool garden, the placement of flowering trees and plants is an achievement in balance and order.

ABOVE: Cushioned loungers with bolster-rolled towels rest in parade formation along the brick-paved patio.

**ABOVE:** Seen from afar, the pergola-shaded patio with its classic furnishings seems to be (and is) an inviting oasis.

**RIGHT:** At the far end of the pool, the coping is adorned with potted topiaries and flowering plants.

**ABOVE:** A dense cover of wisteria on the pergola roof generously shades a dining nook.

**RIGHT:** Striped chaise cushions and cream-colored roses exemplify the overall design palette of white and green.

**BELOW:** On one pool side, the coping abuts the herringbone-patterned brick of the patio.

# STYLE ON A GRAND SCALE

There are many ways to articulate exterior space. In this modern interpretation of classic style, Palm Beach area architect Thierry Despont (designer of both house and pool area) drew his plans on a grand scale.

All of the elements—the roof projecting over the patio, sun umbrellas and furniture, topiaries and planters, modern-art sculptures, even the pool itself—are larger than life-sized.

And yet, because all of the details are so beautifully integrated and balanced, they create a feeling of relaxation. It's as if, for an indefinite period of time, a tastefully decorated public space has been made available for the private enjoyment of you and several dozen of your closest friends—which this space would easily accommodate.

Some of my favorite details include the recurring theme of bougainvillea that tops the poolside sentry box like a toupee, or splashing spikes of color against a circular white wall of the house; the wood and chrome steps leading into the pool-enclosed spa; and the polished wooden bar encircling a tree. At night, the strings of tiny lights wrapped around its branches lend even more enchantment to the parties for which this sumptuous outdoor space is so perfectly suited.

ABOVE: A reclining nude of Rubenesque proportions is one of several outstanding works displayed poolside.

OPPOSITE: The classic elements of balance and order are evident in the furnished patio.

**ABOVE:** In a quiet alcove, a mounted stone of fossils makes an impressive backdrop for stately dining furniture.

**BELOW:** The giant topiary (one of a pair) grows from a custom-made planter of polished epay wood.

**ABOVE:** One end of the pool is generously shaded by nearby trees.

**LEFT:** Thirsty towels filling a shallow square basket are a thoughtful poolside provision for guests.

**ABOVE LEFT:** An exquisite bronze nude is displayed to best advantage on a projecting corner of the pool.

**ABOVE:** A conversational grouping of sofa, chairs, and umbrella-topped table furnish one side of the patio.

**LEFT:** Beautifully crafted of "brick-layered" wood, the bar encircles a light-strung tree that adds magic to the evening.

OPPOSITE, LEFT: A sentry box with a hairpiece of bougainvillea supplies a walk-through "experience" alongside the pool.

OPPOSITE, RIGHT: The teak chaises are so beautiful that even without cushions, they are a great addition to the patio area.

OPPOSITE, BELOW: Not far from the spa, a trio of wooden chaises repose before a towering wall of bougainvillea.

OPPOSITE, BELOW RIGHT: Entertaining is made easy with a multitude of chaises and a nearby bar.

RIGHT: Lush, organic plant materials surround the pool, creating a nice contrast with its sleek structure.

BELOW: A shady limestone patio offers a cool oasis.

BELOW RIGHT: Bougainvillea-topped limestone structures break up the horizontal plane with vertical punctuation and showcase a beautiful ceramic container filled with orchids.

## SUN SHELTERS

For the sake of comfort as well as protection, some form of sun shelter is a must. Umbrellas, the most ubiquitous sunshades, are the most portable. Some varieties open into twelve-foot squares to provide enough shade for a bevy of chaises. Smaller round umbrellas can be used to shade individual chaises or set up in a row to provide coverage for a whole line of chairs. For even more versatility, there are umbrellas with tops that can be adjusted to offer shade whatever the angle of the sun. But as you can see from the photos shown above, your shading options go well past umbrellas. For example, when a patio or terrace is adjacent to the main house or a pool house, a shaded area can be easily created by attaching a structural overhang to it. Or you might consider a retractable awning that gives you the convenient option of sun or shade. (If so, it's recommended that you retract this type of awning during windy weather, which can jostle the framework and jam the retracting mechanism.)

Pergolas are another popular option. Those with a roof construction of closely set lattice strips provide shade while admitting a limited amount of light. Pergolas topped with more widely spaced beams or with open metal gridwork are usually used as an anchorage for vines. Fast-growing varieties

such as climbing clematis, ivy, or wisteria can cover a pergola roof in as little as six months. In the interim, you might want to improvise a temporary sunshade by covering the roof with canvas or straw matting that you've edged with grommets and securely laced to the roof frame.

Of course, the most luxurious sun shelter of all is just that: a shelter. A poolside shelter may come in a number of forms. It might have a peaked roof on column supports and four open sides (rather like a house without walls), or it may be a covered porch reminiscent of an Italian loggia. Some roofed shelters are walled on three sides, the fourth side open to air and light. Some are constructed of wood, others of opaque canvas panels attached to a raised metal framework. Still others might be variations of a Bedouin tent with colorful fabric walls that can be tied back to admit air and light, or completely closed (a nice feature in a sudden summer squall). Aside from their shade-giving properties, however, shelters afford you the wonderful feeling of being indoors and outdoors at the same time. They provide intimacy in a wide-open space. So while you sit in their welcome shade, you don't miss out on the sights, sounds, and scents of the sunny pool and garden areas all around you.

# CLASSIC TRANSFORMATION

When the new owners of an 8-acre property in Greenwich, Connecticut, asked me to redesign the large pool area, I readily understood why: Although the main house overlooking it was 1820s neo-classic, the pool premises were incongruously modern.

The transformation began with the bluestone paving, which was set in a distractingly busy pattern. Since removing it would have been too costly, I reconfigured it and introduced stone walls to subdivide the expanse into a series of cozy outdoor rooms and garden beds. To replace some of the corral fencing, I sandwiched a stretch of metal fencing between English hornbeam hedges, and then covered the pool house with small-scale lattice to create more of an old-world effect.

Because so much was going on visually, new unifying elements were essential. So I decided to pull it all together with color. Directed by the black-and-white scheme of the main house, I used black fiberglass plant boxes to adorn the windows of the pool house, punctuate the four notched corners of the pool, and mark entrances to the various rooms and gardens. I placed black cast-aluminum chairs with white cushions at the poolside, and brought all of the elements together with a black-and-white regency-striped awning to shade the dining porch of the pool house.

During the process, the phrase "symmetry, order, and balance" kept running through my head like a mantra. So how could the result be anything but classic?

OPPOSITE: The vertical lines of oak trees offer a contrast to the horizontal stone wall and help define the entry and exit to the pool area.

ABOVE: A new striped awning gives a Regency air to the refurbished pool house.

**ABOVE:** A boxed palm underplanted with ageratum visually blunts the sharpness of a projecting pool corner.

**ABOVE:** One of the new outdoor spaces—cum fireplace and furnishings— functions as a living room.

**LEFT:** Sill-hung planters and black shutters festoon a window of the restyled pool house.

**OPPOSITE:** Black cast-aluminum chaises with white cushions recline near the pool's curved access steps.

**ABOVE:** A tree of Pee Gee hydrange[a] marks the entrance of a little walled gard[en].

**BELOW:** The refined lines of a scroll-handled urn grace a little stone garden pillar.

**OPPOSITE:** An early-nineteenth-century lantern hangs from the ceiling of [a] pillared porch furnished for conversation[.]

**ABOVE:** The classic style of the dining room pieces is repeated in all the furnishings in the pool area.

# ELEGANT SIMPLICITY

As an undisputed doyenne of the domestic arts, Martha Stewart knows a thing or two about classic design and the effective use of color. Not surprisingly, her pool in East Hampton is an impressive testament to her expertise on both counts.

In this interpretation, classic style achieves a pleasing and intimate simplicity within a space that's comparatively small. Part of that effect comes from an intentionally limited color palette. The predominant scheme is green and blue, ranging

from the warm yellow-green of the shrubs, to the blue-green patio furniture, to the large enamel planters and chaises in Martha's trademark colors of soft green and pale blue.

The clever use of texture and scale is also key. For example, the severe lines of the lap pool's bluestone coping are softened by the weathered red brick pathway that frames it. To play against roughly textured greenery surrounding the pool, there are the smooth enamel surfaces of twin jar planters marking each side of the access steps. Also note that much of the landscaping, though decidedly lush, is confined to knee height or lower so it doesn't overwhelm the confined area of the patio. To add a little drama to the mix (and to introduce more greenery), there's a tiered wooden platform for displaying a whole stageful of potted plants in a way that doesn't take up a lot of space.

The result suggests a restrained elegance and an inviting serenity that exemplifies classic style at its best.

ABOVE: Purple-globed allium injects high-powered color and sculptural interest to a mound of canary-leaved shrubbery.

OPPOSITE: Bricks against bluestone, feathery greens in glossy pots—the play of texture against texture is everywhere.

**ABOVE:** The restrained curlicues of legs and armrests add distinction to simple mesh chairs on a poolside patio.

**ABOVE:** Beneath the kitchen windows, a simply furnished conversation area is bordered by artistically planted flower beds.

**RIGHT:** Two variations of yellow-green plant material play quite nicely against the gray of the bluestone, while providing an architectural element to the space.

**ABOVE:** The variations in shape of the traditional strawberry pot, along with the cool shades of the plant material and warm hues of the container, add visual interest.

**LEFT:** A wooden platform elevates a variety of small-leaved plants unified by their matching celadon green pots.

## GRECIAN REFINEMENT

When notable Palm Beach architect John Volk designed this coastal Florida pool back in 1959, he created a look that's as stylishly relevant today as it was when it was initially built. The unmistakably classic signature is everywhere.

For one thing, the pool is a clean-lined rectangle modified to a notched oval by the curves at each short end. For another, the twin pool houses—with roofs like stair-stepped pyramids—are painted a brilliant Grecian white and symmetrically situated along one of the pool's straight sides. In front of the houses are clipped

swatches of grass with a carpetlike feel— a look that's repeated on the terrace where a pool-sized grass strip is flanked by stone checkerboards, suggesting a natural, outdoor version of the traditional Oriental rug. To further instill a sense of harmony, there's the symmetry of two grape arbor trees—one on each side of the terrace—whose branches meet overhead to frame the entire scene, and beneath each of these, there's a square plinth topped with a suitably classic stone ornament of fruits in a basket.

Aesthetic achievements aside, there are other elements well worth noting, chief among them the panel of sliding glass doors joining the back walls of the double pool house. Those doors not only serve as a security fence but also as a clever windbreak that doesn't obstruct the ocean view.

OPPOSITE: Sinuous branches of a rape arbor tree frame a view of the landscaped patio and curve-ended pool.

ABOVE: Looking like elegant gatehouses, the pool shelters send twin reflections into the still, blue water.

**ABOVE:** The English-style iron bench was designed by Polly Jessup in the 1950s.

**RIGHT:** In a patio corner, chaises are protected from sea winds by a glass wall on their right and a pool house behind.

**LEFT:** Delightful little metal musicians playing along the pool's coping were a housewarming gift to the owner.

LEFT: Though thoroughly landscaped with trees and shrubs, the rectangular pool and patio are wide open to sunlight.

RIGHT: This close-up of a pedestaled stone urn shows the deft detailing of its woven basket and fruit.

BELOW: Green paint on the pool-house shutters is softly echoed on a weathered bench sitting below them.

# NEO-ROMAN TRADITION

In ancient Rome, the very best outdoor baths featured gardens, terraces, and even banquet halls—and architect Audrey Matlock seems to have borrowed from that classical tradition when she designed her own pool in North Haven, New York.

Sited on the lower lawn of her property, the pool is reached from the house by a series of terraces, the focal point of which is an open-sided pavilion with a steeply peaked roof. Beneath its sculptural network of metal crossbeam supports, there's an

appropriately banquet-sized table with enough chairs to seat a legion of guests, along with a kitchen grill and a fireplace to feed them and keep them warm.

Just outside the pavilion, a grass-etched bluestone patio serves as a transitional area to the pool on the lower level, where we find more evidence of classic influence. On one long side of the pool, the garden's flowers and plants are carefully arranged by size, color, and shape. The water of the pool is captured inside a pleasing geometric boundary with horizontals of variegated bluestone for coping and surrounded by a strip of the same variegated stone parqueted to create a walkway. Topping that, in both senses of the word, there's a square bluestone spa designed with an almost industrial simplicity that sends a waterfall cascading into the pool. The effect is as pleasurable to the ear as it is to the eye.

ABOVE: Velvety grids of grass soften the stones of the patio and add their sweet fragrances to the night.

OPPOSITE: The bright reds and yellows of flowering plants shimmer like flames amid the variegated shades of nonflowering greens.

**ABOVE:** From the vantage point of the spa, the viewer's eye sweeps over shelter, pool, and garden bed.

**RIGHT:** From the dining table, the open-walled construction of the shelter reveals views of gardens, patio, and lawn.

**OPPOSITE:** On a cool summer evening, a crackling fire and a prettily set table await dinner guests in the shelter.

# A COUNTRY CLASSIC

When landscape architect Judy Murphy and her husband decided to install a pool on their Lakeville, Connecticut, property, there wasn't any question about placement: The only available spot was in between some trees and a barn. Now what they have is a lovely marsite pool with the barn porch serving as the pool house.

In structure, the layout is decidedly formal, but in Judy's personal interpretation of classic, the materials are earthy and rustic. At one end of the pool, the symmetry of two old-growth trees is echoed at the opposite end by a pair of antique cast-iron Corinthian columns. The security fence surrounding the pool is a primitive New England fieldstone wall that becomes a kind of wainscoting beneath a wooden arbor cornice covered with grape vines—a configuration that not only meets code requirements, but also gives the pool area the aesthetically satisfying feel of an enclosed room.

If you look closely, you'll see minute details you may be tempted to re-create yourself, such as the double slabs of bluestone that not only act as the pool's coping but also provide seating around it.

For the Murphy family, the pool is a focal point for recreation, exercise, and entertaining. And sometimes it's just a relaxing retreat for watching the play of light and shade on the water.

OPPOSITE: Though the pool is small in size, its serene setting and open-arched wall create an illusion of spaciousness.

ABOVE: Enormous columns, originally used at a Philadelphia train station, make a dramatic statement.

# THE POWER OF COLOR

There's an aesthetic satisfaction about this pool in Dutchess County, New York—a kind of moving narrative as you pass from place to place. It begins as you descend from one lawn-carpeted terrace to the next, stepping down one series of steps and then onto another flanked by flower-filled urns marking it as the main access to the centerpiece: a calm expanse of aquamarine water.

This is classic with a capital *C,* and one of its unifying themes is color. The rich green grass, the vine-covered pergola, and the trees that encircle the outer ring of these enclosures within enclosures become even more striking as they are played against the pristine white stone of the patio-terrace columns on one side of the pool and the long gated wall on another.

Because the pool area was designed as a recreational and entertaining space for a family with several grandchildren, its luxurious formality loosens up to provide plenty of tables and chairs arranged in groupings beneath the shady pergola for casual lunches and elaborate dinner parties. Between swimming sessions, those spacious lawns might become playgrounds or a croquet court, and behind the wall there's the hidden surprise of a waterslide that delights the adults just as much as it does the kids.

ABOVE: Statuary like this appealing Venus and baby Cupid is a traditional element of classic style.

OPPOSITE: Stone griffins on carved columns and a scrolled iron gate make a lovely frame for this view of the pool.

OVERLEAF: A vine-drenched pergola and the white brickwork of stairs and walls conjure a villa in ancient Greece.

# FOUNTAINS AND WATER FEATURES

When most people think of Rome, one of the first images that comes to mind is that great city's wealth of glorious fountains. The genius of these works lies not only in their beauty as sculptural art, but in the fact that the sculptures are also fountains. Clearly, Bernini and company understood their public's eternal fascination with moving water—the lure of it, the sight of it, and of course, the sound of it.

Charles Dickens once referred to a fountain's playful sound as "liquid music"—a perfect description. Add to that the beguiling movement of the water as it spurts upward or arcs over the pool, and it's easy to understand why fountains and other water features are fast becoming standard elements in pool design.

The basic mechanism of fountains, jets,

and the like will recycle water through a circulating pump. Such contrivances can be configured to produce a number of effects. You could center a fountain in the pool via pipes attached to the pool floor. Jets of water shooting out from a series of decorative tiles in the pool's side walls create another attractive display. For a modern setting, a fountain could be a set of simple

metal pipes trickling water into a trough; for a romantic one, it could be an old-world font set into the grottolike niche of a wall.

On the other hand, your fountain may be a free-standing sculptural piece—anything from a magnificently-tiled Moorish fantasy to a simple stone plinth-and-trough recalling the ancient water structures in little village squares throughout the Mediterranean—that takes pride of place on a poolside patio. Finally, there's the granddaddy of all water features: the waterfall (which, come to think of it, was probably the original inspiration for fountains in the first place). If you've always wanted one of your own, there are fabricated versions that can be rigged into the roof of a poolside shelter or covered patio so that the press of a button releases a cataract of water into the pool. In fact, you can even mimic nature itself by installing one that gushes down over a man-made precipice of greenery and splashes over rocks into the pool below. When properly done by a talented designer, these natural-looking waterfalls can convincingly provide the same visual and musical magic as the real thing and offer a much-needed vertical to a horizontal space.

# LUXURIOUS LEISURE

Shaped like an elongated Roman arch, this Jamaican pool seems to shoot out from the hillside that faces Montego Bay. The promontory is called Round Hill, and it's the setting for a private enclave of luxury homes-cum-clubhouses built on terraces descending the lushly planted slope to the water below. This particular pool and house, sited at the very top of the hill, belongs to Round Hill's resident manager.

Designed in an understated form of classical style, nothing here is done to excess—a wonderful ploy that allows the viewer to focus on the beauty and quality of the comparatively few decorative elements.

For example, the unfurnished patio surrounding the pool is laid with squares of stone set on the diagonal and connected with a traditional diamond pattern of small stones. That same medium is used to embellish the risers of a turquoise-painted iron-railed stairway curving up to the elevated porch overlooking the pool and its magnificent backdrop. Even there, the furnishings (a chaise, a sofa,  and several round tables) are few in number. Since the furnishings happen to be made of exquisite, antique Victorian wicker, little else is needed for style or comfort.

Other classical details are just as simple, like the sparsely rendered circular design on the porch's iron railing, the touches of white in the furniture cushions, and the style of the surrounding fence. Simplify, simplify, and if the elements are right, you'll find that less really can be more.

OPPOSITE: The pool water repeats the turquoise hue of Jamaica's Montego Bay.

ABOVE: On an open porch, the antique patina of the Victorian furniture aptly expresses the prevailing mood of relaxed classicism.

OPPOSITE: Small details—a turquoise railing, risers embedded with colored stones—turn a simple stairway into something spectacular.

RIGHT: The introduction of an ocher clay pot creates a decorative contrast to the blue-gray hues of the stairs and patio.

BELOW: The abstract sunburst is a section of iron railing on the porch overlooking the pool.

RUSTIC

# THE RUSTIC POOL

Natural. Unstructured. Unpretentious. These are the characteristics of rustic style. In design terms, it means that the pool itself is usually free- form in shape or edged with stones or rocks so that

it seems to merge with the landscape, whether that setting was crafted by nature or deliberately planted to look that way. Even the pool's lining may be a dark shade so that the water will mimic the coloring of a pond or a lagoon.

A rustic pool shelter will often be constructed from stone or logs to blend in with its natural surroundings, its wooden columns still bristling with bits of bark. It may even have a pinecone-riddled pediment. Inside the shelter and on the patio, furniture will often be rough-hewn, unpainted, and countrified.

In other words, at its most successful, the rustic-style pool makes you feel as if you've somehow managed to discover a natural paradise and claim it for your own—which is exactly why so many people love it.

ABOVE: In rustic idiom, patio would mean a backyard lawn, furnishings, a tree-slung hammock and folding chairs.

OPPOSITE: Here, rustic style is a free-form pool landscaped with rocks and look-of-the-wild flowers.

## PRIMITIVE ELEGANCE

It's not surprising that renowned interior designer Bunny Williams has imprinted her own inimitable stamp on the pool she designed for her property in northwestern Connecticut, where she and her husband, John Rosselli, get to enjoy the best of both worlds: modern conveniences informed by a distinctively rustic mien.

For example, the pool shelter—a primitive wooden temple with a pinecone pediment and tree trunks doubling as Doric columns—serves as repository not only for dining and living room furniture but also for a minikitchen complete with grill, a limestone fireplace, a bathroom, and an outdoor shower.

The granite pool is a linear size (15 by 36 feet, perfect for short laps), with access steps running along one side for seating. The smooth coping is disguised with chunky seventeenth-century stones transported from a basin in France. The patio area is made of grass and furnished with a quartet of Sunbrella-cushioned wooden chaises. Even the sun umbrellas reflect the Williams touch: They're mushroom-shaped woven disks supported by thick bamboo poles. Temple-like, the shelter is open-sided except for an elegant back wall featuring a fireplace and sitting/dining areas.

From its Olympian height looking down on the village below, this elegant back-country setting could easily be imagined as the kind of place a family of Greek gods might have chosen for a weekend getaway.

OPPOSITE: Granite coping raised above grade becomes a sitting wall around the pool.

ABOVE: Glass-shaded candles, a modeled stag, and a filigreed medallion top the mantel of a huge limestone fireplace.

**ABOVE:** Beside the small pool, the shelter, furnishings, even stones on the coping, are all fashioned on a massive scale.

**LEFT:** Bamboo furniture in the open living room area is rustic style at its best (i.e., rugged and handsome).

**ABOVE LEFT:** The shelter's interior wall—weathered wainscoting beneath hand-painted canvas—supplies the background for a country chair.

**ABOVE:** The primitive wooden cage is Williams's amusingly clever take on a plant holder.

**LEFT:** The bathroom has a bowl for a sink, a hanging lantern for light—and full marks for charm.

**BELOW:** A multitude of small terra-cotta containers filled with luscious plants offers an intimate touch.

# RUSTIC RETREAT

A small woodland of old-growth trees provides the perfect setting for this rustic pool in northern New Jersey. Sited at the edge of a meadow and a distance away from the main house, it's a private retreat for the owners, who prize its tranquillity.

The pool might best be described as a geometric shape that breaks into free form—which is wonderfully in keeping with the easy and often whimsical rustic

character. The coping, along with the subtle suggestion of a patio, is made of hefty chunks of rock (called greiss), which are loosely pieced together with creeping thyme and other greens poking through the spaces in between.

Resting beneath the canopy of a tree are a pair of casual flea market–look chaises that don't necessarily reside there on a permanent basis but simply end up wherever poolside loungers decide to place them. Underneath a nearby tree is a bench, and in the neighboring

shelter is an unpretentious table and chair set used for casual dining.

With its open sides and shallow-peaked roof, the shelter itself is a cross between a lean-to and a pool house. A long stretch of rough-hewn stone steps leads to a vine-covered pergola that provides a welcome respite from the sun. Another touch of whimsy can be seen on the shelter's back clapboard wall: What looks like an open window is really a mirror reflecting the nearby trees.

ABOVE: For this version of rustic, the rough-hewn look of the pool shape and the patio stones were essential architectural ploys.

OPPOSITE: A pair of old metal chaises on the lawn typifies the unpretentious appeal of the pool's relaxed, laid-back style.

## VISION OF PARADISE

No, it's not an island in Tahiti but a tropical paradise carved from a mere hanky-sized property in Miami's Coconut Grove. The genius behind the illusion is Mark Ingmire, a landscape architect whose specialty is creating pool settings in the rustic-gone-native style you see here.

The shape of the pool is the ultimate example of free form, framed by judicious placements of towering palms, graceful ferns, and other subtropical greenery that spill onto the surface of the water. (In fact, this is actually a no-maintenance freshwater pool, free-flowing and pure enough to drink.)

The rest of the pool's perimeter is taken up by a primitive wooden deck patio—a meandering pathway suspended right above the water line to double as a diving platform. The patio has a palm-thatched roof supported by fantastically shaped driftwood columns, thus creating a shaded front porch for the house to which it's attached. Inside the roof is another surprise: With the push of a button, a cascade of water is released into the pool.

Patio furnishings—a weathered bench or two and an inviting hammock—are as casually rustic as the rest. Even an unfinished chest of drawers and a mirror reflecting lush greenery don't seem the least bit out of place here. Seeing it for the first time, you feel as if you've stumbled upon the lagoon-side hut of an island native who just happens to have a very nice sense of style.

**OPPOSITE:** Sunlight glinting through lush tropical growth warms the lagoonlike waters of the pool.

**ABOVE:** A wonderful, shaded dining spot is found poolside.

**RIGHT:** This decorative macrame piece echoes the cascade of the waterfall in the background.

**BELOW:** This flowering plant is so incredible, it's hard to believe it's real. It's strikingly similar to a piece of ornate jewelry.

**RIGHT:** From one roofed section of the patio deck, a viewer enjoys the sight of a man-made waterfall.

RIGHT: This slatted wood entryway is beautifully framed by gorgeous plant material, giving the sense that one is entering a true outdoor room.

ABOVE: The owner's dog enjoys the same swimming privileges as humans and fish.

BELOW: Colorful varieties of freshwater fish glimmer beneath the surface of the lagoon.

# RELAXING RUSTICATIONS

Designed by landscape architect Christopher LaGuardia, this pool can be seen from the back porch of a little two-bedroom cottage situated at the bottom of a grassy slope. Although the Sag Harbor, New York, property is only a third of an acre in size, its waterside location makes it feel as though it extends all the way to the opposite shore of the Peconic Bay. The natural setting also helps to establish the rusticism of the pool, which is a 15-by-35-foot rectangle used for swimming laps and

as a soothing focal point during predinner cocktails on the lawn. What makes it particularly interesting is the random placement of rock slabs and boulders along the concrete coping, the color of which echoes that of the natural rocks surrounding it. Additional sculptural elements include a copse of assorted trees (which also serve to screen the pool from next-door neighbors) and irises, hydrangeas, roses, hostas, and catnip.

Like so many rustic pools, this one is surrounded by grass in place of a more structured patio. Again, pool furniture is minimal: a pair of simply designed chaises and an inviting hammock slung between two fortuitously placed trees. When guests drop in, somebody just drags down a couple of old metal lawn chairs that are normally found a little farther up the slope—because the thing about rustic is, it's not just a style; it's an attitude.

ABOVE: In back of the cottage, a down-home-style porch sits above the pool and its grass patio.

OPPOSITE: The natural adornments of sculptural trees, a rock, and a frame of lawn complement the pool's honest simplicity.

**ABOVE:** Chairs (both folding and '50s-type) are cozily arranged for enjoying the pleasing vista of pool and bay.

**LEFT:** Lichen-filmed boulders artfully placed along the bluestone coping rusticate the structured lines of the pool.

**OPPOSITE, ABOVE:** For this relaxed, countrified setting, a tree-slung hammock is mandatory.

**OPPOSITE, BELOW:** House-at-the-lake–style pieces furnish the cottage's screened porch.

## BEDS

Although a bed isn't the first thing you might think about in relation to furnishing a patio area, some people (myself included) regard it as the perfect poolside addition. After all, what you want to do most around a pool is relax, and how better to do that than by stretching out on a bed? An outdoor bed is a great place for reading or even for eating—especially if it accommodates some kind of

canopy to shade you from the sun.

Since a poolside bed is usually treated as a permanent fixture, you'll naturally want one that's made of rustproof metal or a weatherproof wood with a mattress and pillows that are water- and stain-resistant. Even more vulnerable varieties, such as antique wooden beds, are wonderful furnishings for an enclosed pool house, which can then

double as sleeping quarters for guests.

Other bed-furnishing options for a pool shelter might include an attractive cot-like bed on a fixed wooden frame with carved legs, or a daybed railed on three sides and adorned with colorful throw pillows to provide comfortable group seating by day and accommodate a single sleeper at night. When it comes to choosing a bed—whether

you intend to place it inside a shelter, right next to the pool, or even in a garden or outdoor room adjacent to the pool/patio area—it might pay to think outside the box spring. That is, since the beds you're likely to find in orthodox furniture stores are designed for indoor conditions, check out less conventional sources, like furniture shops specializing in imports from such places as India,

Indonesia, and other warm-weather spots where rooms are often open to the outdoors.

Or you could scour thrift shops and flea markets (or even your own attic) for a funky old iron bed that you won't be afraid to leave outdoors. And don't forget outdoor-furnishings places, which sometimes carry extra-wide chaises that convert into double beds. A group of beds provides an alternative

to traditional outdoor seating. In addition to sitting or lounging on outdoor beds, some people like the idea of sleeping on them at night. If you agree, it's best to choose a canopied bed style (or one with head- and footboards, or high corner posts) to support a swath of protective mosquito netting. A final thought: Pets enjoy poolside naps too, so why not include bedding for them as well?

## COTSWOLD IN THE HAMPTONS

One look at the splendid appointments and landscaping tells you that this swimming pool plays an important role in the lives of the people who use it. In fact, when the owners first bought this property in New York's Hamptons, they had the pool area built even before blueprints for the main house were drawn up, which resulted in the main house being designed to follow the same style as the romantic, rustic pool.

The most obvious expressions of the pool's style are the twin cottages that serve as pool houses. Details like peaked slate roofs, colonial greenstone quoins cornering white-washed walls, and mullioned windows with lush flower boxes suggest the kind of country cottages found in the Cotswolds.

Filling the space between the two pool houses is a patio that's partially shaded by a wooden pergola and furnished as an outdoor living room complete with cast-metal chairs and coffee tables painted a soft celadon green. What I especially like about this patio is the irregular bluestone flooring and wide, curved steps that lead up to it. Even though the steps are low and not much higher than the pool level, they're all that's needed to elevate the space like a stage setting and add another element of subtle architectural interest.

Other examples of attention to detail include the free-form pool that echoes the shape of a natural pond and, ascending from it, the spectacular rock gardens and waterfalls that guide the eye to a higher level of beautifully variegated trees (a perfect backdrop for the rustic setting they enclose).

OPPOSITE: Overhanging trees add their verdant beauty to the lavishly landscaped rock garden and waterfall.

ABOVE: In the foreground of the slate-roofed shelters, a spa hugs the pool like an elongated coin.

OPPOSITE, ABOVE: One of the twin shelters conveniently houses pool equipment; the other is a bath-cum-changing room.

OPPOSITE, BELOW: Turquoise metal furnishings on the patio intentionally duplicate the water color of the pool.

ABOVE: Within the free-form shape of the pool, opposing arcs of coping create two water-washed bridges.

LEFT: Purple petunias and maidenhair ferns spill over the window box of a cottage shelter.

RIGHT: The convincing arrangement of rocks and plants in the garden is an impressive example of artful artifice.

**ABOVE:** The overflow from a basin onto slanted layers of stone plays its own special water music in the garden.

**RIGHT:** Behind the patio, a wisteria-framed wall fountain contributes a European flavor to its rural surroundings.

**OPPOSITE:** In another pool area, a double-tiered cataract pours a sheet of water into the depths of the pool.

# PEACEFUL PRIVACY

Given the right spin, even unlikely elements can be adapted to the laid-back rustic style—as is demonstrated on this property in northwestern Connecticut. Here the pool area (a fair distance from the house) is sited on a high rise of land against a stand of trees and overlooking a lush valley that spreads out like a patchwork quilt below.

Since the original idea was to create a private spa where the owners could swim

laps, do yoga, or just unwind with a good book, they chose a simple linear pool measuring 50 by 12 feet with a short, squared-off extension on one side to provide pool access and keep guests from getting in the way of someone swimming laps. To rusticate the sharp rectilinear shape of the pool, they coped it with natural bluestone and bordered it with grass.

Wide stairs of weather-aged wood lead away from the pool and approach a screened-in shelter. With its unadorned wooden pillars and primitively rendered pagoda roof, the exotic architectural gesture achieves a Zenlike simplicity. In keeping with that mood, furnishings are kept to a minimum. At two corners of the pool are oversized clay jars (originally used to store oil). Inside the shelter, there's little more than a pair of Indian string beds covered with pillows. Several baskets holding yoga mats and such are stored underneath. For sitting or lying in the sun, the shelter's grass-treaded wooden steps serve just as well as any conventional poolside chaise.

ABOVE: Sun-splashed trees on a nearby slope produce a natural wall mural behind the shelter's simple furnishings.

OPPOSITE: The restrained lines of the screened pavilion are perfectly partnered by the clean, chiseled shape of the pool.

# PLANT CONTAINERS

In pool-design terms, the solid flooring and man-made furnishings of the patio are called hardscaping. Containers filled with flowers and plants add the necessary softening touch to these rigid surfaces by introducing natural garden elements in a variety of interesting textures, shapes, and colors.

A plant container might be a vase, an urn, or a ceramic or stone jar. It can be a simple cement planter shaped like a salad bowl. It can be earth-toned (like terra-cotta), enameled with melding shades of a single color, or elaborately painted with rich geometric designs whose colors might be used to match or coordinate the pool area's color theme. As for size, the bigger the better: Whatever container you choose should be large enough to stand out and hold its own against the patio's expanse. It should also be large enough to comfortably hold (and allow growing room for) whatever's inside it, which may include anything from a lush minigarden of flowers and greens to a 6-foot-high palm tree.

And while we're on the subject of outsized containers—particularly the type of pots and jars used for larger plants or trees—it's usually a good idea to raise the container a bit above ground level to facilitate drainage. To do this, you could place the container on a bed of stones, or choose the

kind of jar or pot that fits into a footed holder. Also, if you're placing a large, heavy plant on a grass patio or other lawn area, resting it on its own square of cement (like a permanent coaster) will not only lend authority to the potted plant, but also keep it from crushing the grass. The cement will also absorb the drainage water so the grass around it stays dry. But "bigger is better" doesn't mean that smaller (sometimes very small) plant contain-

ers don't have their place in the scheme of things. For example, displaying a collection of small-to-medium sized potted plants all clustered together in a single area could have the same visual impact as a single oversized plant container. Some tricks for making it work: To give the display a sense of unity, choose various sizes of smaller terracotta pots that are all the same shape, or glazed pots that are all the same color. To

give your collection importance, elevate it on a stepped platform, or on little pedestals of differing heights. Other container types include wrought-iron structures or, for a more modern look, simply designed brushed-steel pots. Wooden containers are another viable option. They could take the form of free-standing tubs or troughs, or window boxes attached to a pool house or, for that matter, any wall with windows that abuts the patio.

# PHOTO CREDITS

# INDEX